THE HIGH STAKES GAME

OF FATHERHOOD

KNOW
WHEN
TO
HOLD
'EM

JOHN BLASE

Abingdon Press

Nashville

KNOW WHEN TO HOLD 'EM
THE HIGH STAKES GAME OF FATHERHOOD

For Will, Sarah, and Abbey

Library of Congress Cataloging-in-Publication Data has been requested.

ISBN 978-1-4267-5821-8

13 14 15 16 17 18 19 20 21 22—10 9 8 7 6 5 4 3 2

MANUFACTURED IN THE UNITED STATES OF AMERICA

CONTENTS

USUALLY THEY ARE NOT EXPERTS: *their ambitions and fantasies are strong enough to brush aside the doubts which more cautious men might have. Determination and faith are their strongest weapons. At best such men are regarded as eccentric; at worst, mad. . . .*

Everest has attracted its share of men like these. Their mountaineering experience varied from none at all to very slight—certainly none of them had the kind of experience which would make an ascent of Everest a reasonable goal. Three things they all had in common: faith in themselves, great determination, and endurance.

—*Walt Unsworth,* Everest

INTRODUCTION

✦✦✦✦✦✦✦✦✦

MAY 10, 1996. 57 HOURS WITHOUT sleep. 29,028 feet. As Jon Krakauer used his hands as he struggled to make his descent down Mount Everest, little did he know those same hands would soon type the definitive account of the deadliest season in the history of Mount Everest—*Into Thin Air*. Krakauer could have waited seasons before writing his book, allowing the dust to settle on his experience into a reflected wisdom. Several authors and editors counseled him to pause for perspective. But as sound as that advice may have been, he ignored it. He wrote immediately, with the raw prose of one who was just there—a witness.

February 10, 1997. Not quite 15 hours without sleep. 299 feet. My hands struggled to cut the umbilical cord that attached my firstborn son to his mother. It took me two tries, but I did it. I did it again on July 13, 1998, and a final time on March 22, 2003. I could wait until I'm old and gray to write about fathering these three children, allowing an acceptable sifting of my memory. But I will not; in some sense I cannot. I want to write in the real-time prose of one who is there, smack dab in the middle of possibly the greatest summit attempt of my life—being a dad. I want to witness.

An obvious question here is why? Why do I feel compelled to witness? Krakauer wrote because his summit attempt came with the death of his companions. At the risk of sounding dramatic, I see a similar "terrible cost" as our culture continues to view fathers as either unnecessary fools or indispensable saviors; both extremes are burdens too heavy to bear, both are slowly killing us. I am writing because I want to try and help and the only way I know to do that is to tell stories in such a way as to say "here's what I saw or did; what do you think?" To that end each chapter concludes with a thought to spur your own thoughts and maybe in that conversation, together, we can thrive, we can do well. I do believe this is possible, so while this is a book about fathering, it is also a book about hope, that with faith, great determination, and endurance, we can do this.

The author John Updike wrote, "My father provided; he gathered things to himself and let them fall upon the world; my clothes, my food, my luxurious hopes had fallen to me from him."[1] I like that phrase—"luxurious hopes." It has nothing to do with one's socioeconomic status; it is something much more substantive than that, something that I pray is stirred in you as you read these pages.

✦✦✦✦✦✦✦✦✦

When the doctor handed me the scissors to cut the umbilical cord there were no words exchanged between us other than the unspoken communication of man to man, the language of look, nod, gesture. As I took the instrument from his hand, his eyes told me, *This is your move. You cut him loose.* So I did. My wife had pushed and groaned and rocked for hours, willing this firstborn son into the world. Now he was here, finally, but he was still tethered to her via that ropy cord. I had to cut him loose. So I did. I repeated that move when our daughters were born as well. It seemed this intrinsically irrational act, but there's no other phrase that accurately captures the feel of those seconds, those cutting loose moments when I set my children free into this world. Did I fully understand what was going on in those emancipations? No, but I did have an awareness that the ante was suddenly raised, there was no room for bluff. I acknowledged that this was something that had to be done regardless of what would follow.

What followed has been and continues to be one of the most exhilarating, risky, frustrating, and challenging experiences of my life. I have quickly seen there are no guarantees, no fail-safe routes to raising daughters and sons. Anyone who tells you differently or writes a book that tells you differently is a liar. Like attempting to climb Everest, fathering is a triumph of desire over sensibility, something I believe all men hold in common.

One note. You will notice the use of religious language from time to time. It is here for two reasons. First, trying to be a father, like trying to scale Everest, is a religious act. There is something about this endeavor that is different in kind from changing your tires or filing your taxes. It requires faith, and with that admittance we are instantly in the realm of the sacred. Second, however anachronistic I may be I am a product of a religious America that quite honestly does not exist anymore. I've accepted that, but to betray the language of where I've been would be to import some nicety that in the final analysis is good for nothing.

I may not know who I am,
but I know where I am from.
—Wallace Stegner

FIRSTS AND SECONDS

In some sense, yes,
it is a season full of firsts:
the first time you feel his skin
or hear her sneeze
or smell her toes
or catch him smile.
Yes, that is the sense.
But love of an infant is of a different order—
it is only seconds.
Tuck them all away inside you
for one day, far from now,
they will help you pass the time.

ONE

THE WORK OF YOUR HANDS

✦✦✦✦✦✦✦✦✦

Linger.

—*Jack Gilbert*

My YOUNGEST DAUGHTER, Abbey, looked at me this afternoon and asked, "Are you thinking what I'm thinking?" She's four. I said, "Yes" and winked at her; she winked back and returned to what she was thinking about. I have no idea what that was. But I wish I did.

What was she thinking about in that moment? What was going on behind those saddle-brown eyes with falling auburn hair in them? I've been home quite a bit lately; I have some writing deadlines and so many days have found me in the basement, in front of a keyboard, from last star to first. She's four, so she's been home as well. She's come down to check on me quite often, she doesn't stay long, just a little while.

Although I hear her coming down the stairs, she is convinced she's sneaking up on me and greets me with a "boo" and I do my best startle and she always says, "It's me, Abbey." Many days she wants to go to a "dot-com" and print off coloring pages from the My Little Pony or Curious George websites. Even at four years old she displays a persistence that I believe will carry her far in this life. So we usually sit and wait for my printer to start its heaving, eventually coughing up pictures for her to color. I've noticed on the last few visits that she has put her hand on my arm while presenting her case. I wonder what she's thinking about. I hope she's thinking that her dad is so happy when she sneaks down the stairs to startle him. That he's so relieved it's her, Abbey, whose name means "father's joy." I hope she's thinking that it's a good thing for her to put her hand on my arm and reassure her dad that his work these days in not in vain, although most days he's not sure, driving his family in a metaphorical covered wagon across uncertain terrain in search of his dreams to be a writer.

I pray she's thinking that asking me for coloring pages will help me keep some childlikeness in my afternoons that frequently border on the serious and anxious. I hope she's thinking, *I'll stand close enough to Dad so he can smell my hair. He helped me wash it last night and that'll make him remember the true work of his hands these days—fathering.*

He's got plenty of time to be a writer, but his days of fathering are numbered. I'm four, but not for long.

And maybe that was what she was thinking about this afternoon when she asked me if I knew what she was thinking about. "I'm growing up, Daddy, fast." Today it's dot-coms and "boo" and the man with the yellow hat, but tomorrow it'll be girlfriends and boys and talking on the phone into the wee small hours of the morning and saying, "Dad, please," when I stop and smell her hair.

I have no idea what my little girl's thoughts are; many days I can't even fathom my own. But in the precision of this moment I am grateful for her hand on my arm, and for her reminder that it is not a small thing when a child loves you.

In this moment that's what I'm thinking about.

Children have the gift of startling us awake
to the true work of our hands. Linger.

TWO

RESPONSE-ABLE FATHERING

✦✦✦✦✦✦✦✦✦

We knew an intimacy had
bloomed between us.

—*Gretel Ehrlich*

I CAME HOME FROM WORK today and my nine-year-
old son met me at the door with a song about vaginas. Yes,
I typed that correctly. I let him sing it and then asked him
where he heard that word. I immediately sensed the potential
for shame rising in the room, so I quickly told him he wasn't
in trouble but that he and I probably oughta talk about that

word. Too often we react to things with our children and fly off the handle (now that's a descriptive phrase) and there's nothing left to feel in that space but shame. But we are able to respond—response-able—and that is something altogether different, and altogether harder.

It came out that somebody named Seth taught him the song at school. When I asked him if he knew what vagina meant, he pointed to his chest. The song's lyrics were along the lines of "Boys have small vaginas and girls have big ones . . ." I'm not the sharpest knife in the drawer but based on that snippet I reckoned we were actually talking about breasts. I'm not overly thrilled about Seth lifting the skirt on sex for my son. However, it happens that way, like it or not. For all our efforts to be proactive in every regard, it doesn't always work out that way. And maybe sometimes it's best if it doesn't because it allows us to grow alongside our children.

When I was in second grade I didn't have a friend named Seth, but I did know a boy named Marcus. His skin was as black as mine is white. Marcus wore a commanding Afro and walked with a physicality I'm just now coming into at thirty-nine. I will never forget that day in the boy's bathroom when Marcus pulled out a picture that he had to unfold several times, a sort of reverse Russian nesting doll moment. He motioned for me to come close. What gradually unfolded was a woman whose skin was as black as mine was white but who didn't have a stitch of clothes on to save her life.

I recall some level of arousal in that moment, probably due to the fact that it was something we were doing in secret hushed-boy-bathroom tones. The sexual aspect of the image was overwhelming—I'd never seen anything like that or those before. And then the moment collapsed, some other boys came in and Marcus quickly put a wrap on the goods. We returned to the innocence of the playground, where teachers stood like heroes at the boundaries and girls were skipping rope in white Keds and red-rovered boys kept calling on wimpy guys to "come over."

I don't know what all I'll say to my son in regard to the song he learned today. But we'll stumble through as fathers and sons do. I'll tell him about Marcus and hopefully he'll tell me a little more about Seth. But we won't have our talk in the bathroom; no, I've decided we'll go outside and swing— talk about grown-up matters while doing a childlike thing. I'll try and bring some clarity to the breast/vagina difference; shouldn't be too difficult. I'll more than likely tell him that Seth is full of bologna, like little Marcus was; boys trying to be men too fast, too soon, pre-mature. Maybe my son will ask me questions. If so, I'll try and answer them. I may not be able to, though, because I may not know the answers and if that's the case, then we'll stand in that unashamed space and I'll say, "Let's figure that out together."

Then again maybe he'll be satisfied with a succinct biology lesson and say, "OK, Now can we swing some more?" And if that's the case I'll breathe a little easier because vaginas and breasts and the electrifying mystery of sex will wait, not forever, but for just a little longer while I stand behind my son and push him higher and higher. Then I'm sure he'll say, "I got it, Dad." And I'll back up and watch him reach for the sky as geese honk overhead and the chain bounces beneath his weight.

Maybe as he swings I'll hum a little tune myself, a collection of notes I'll assemble from the moment, a song of the boy on the edge of his quest, swinging back to me for strength and clarity about powerful things then swinging away from me into the world of boys like Seth eager to be men, and girls who skip rope in white Keds.

As I envision that moment in my head I like my placement; I am behind him. I don't want to get in the way of his story playing itself out because it's his story, not mine. But I want to be there, close by, close enough to respond and for him to hear me singing "swing away, swing away."

Reactions tend to shut our children down.
But a response keeps the story going,
and that's what we all really want.

THREE

CHANCEY FAITH

✦✦✦✦✦✦✦✦✦

Courage is the ability to cultivate a relationship with the unknown.

—*David Whyte*

DO YOU KNOW WHAT'S unknown in our lives? Everything. And this unknown piece is compounded by several powers of ten when it comes to raising kids, mainly because you've got all these unknowns in your own life and then all of a sudden you have one or more other lives filling up with their own unknowns. It can just about drown you some days.

I don't know very many parents who like Lemony Snicket's *A Series of Unfortunate Events*. They find it too dark and depressing and weird. But it's a favorite of mine. It's not that I like unfortunate happenings necessarily; it's that I believe the story is a lot closer to the reality in which we find ourselves. Sometimes the check doesn't arrive or the acceptance letter gets lost or you lose your job or your savings or your home or your parents. Was there a chance those things could've happened? Sure, but you just never thought they actually would come to pass.

I find it odd that the words *chance* and *faith* are rarely heard in the same breath. I find this especially odd in religious circles as the definition of faith is "the essence of things unseen"—in other words, there's a lotta unknown here. Most days you can't see what's going on to save your life, but hey, take a *chance*, step on out there in, well, *faith*. We can blather on all we want about knowing "the rest of the story" and go through life a bunch of smiling Paul Harveys when just below the surface we're terrified.

The subtitle to this book is "The High Stakes Game of Fatherhood." That about says it. It's high stakes, all of it, and there are days when the milk and honey flow and there are days when the disappointment is an unsolvable riddle. The Bible verse from my youth said to "work out your salvation with fear and trembling" (Philippians 2:12 NIV). Now you can take that and become a Chicken-Little-the-sky-is-falling parent or you could become a gambler of sorts, a father or a mother, aunt or grandfather, who keeps coming back to the table, day in, day out, not knowing what's going to happen but courageous enough to keep playing the game. And realizing at some point that the goal is not so much winning the game as learning to play well, even enjoying the risk.

Now some might call this being shrewd, a smooth operator. I call it being a person of courage, someone working out his or her life with a roll-of-the-dice faith. And always hoping for the best, always.

Being a parent is the epitome of the unknown.
Be-friending the unknown won't make it all better,
but it can make for quite the game.

FOUR

STAY CLOSE

✦✦✦✦✦✦✦✦

No matter how far the low tide goes out, . . .

the high tide always comes

in again as high as ever.

—*Frederick Buechner*

I CHECKED ON OUR GIRLS last night before I went to
bed. They had finally fallen asleep after several water runs, a
quick check to see who got booted off *Dancing with the Stars*,
and some last minute giggling. My check on them is routine:

turn off their radio, make sure they're covered up, and switch off the night-light.

Our youngest, Abbey, had crawled over in the bed with Sarah (they have twin beds bumped up against each other) and I was going to pull her back over in her bed. But something stopped me. When I bent down to lift Abbey over, I noticed the girls' arms were intertwined. I followed the arms to the hands and finally to the fingers. My two little girls, my fathers-be-good-to-your-daughters daughters were asleep holding hands with their fingers interlaced. I backed up and just looked at them. I stepped across the hall and whispered to my wife: "Come see this." And there we stood, arm in arm, awed at the wonder of it all.

We spent some time last night watching a little (*a little,* mind you) of the coverage of the Virginia Tech shooting. I asked the kids if their teachers had said anything about it at school and they said no. I didn't expect a day-long symposium on the event, but I did feel like the teachers owed the kids at least a nod to this tragedy. We didn't force the kids to sit still and watch the evening news; they came and went as they pleased. But we did answer any questions they had and made some comments at points in the report. We cringed at images of lives cut short by a "cold" shooter and were disappointed at a reporter's insatiable quest for the answer to "how did you feel?"

Our son watched intently, but the girls maintained an ebb and flow, playing in their rooms for a while then returning to the den for a few minutes, then back to Play-Doh and dolls. I do wonder if the girls saw and heard more than I realized. In the splendor of their innocence, maybe they could stand just a little and then had to return to the safety of play.

Maybe. I don't know for sure. All I know is that it sure felt like the final thing they did before surrendering to sleep last night was to lock arms and hold hands, fingers and all, to scrunch up next to each other, as close as possible, and hang on. They were entering the night, where things are dark and shadowy and alma maters can become lessons of grief in the twinkling of an eye.

I'm certain the next few days will hold what we refer to as "processing the tragedy." I'm sure experts will tell us what we're feeling is normal, although the word *normal* seems so out of place. Seeing my girls last night challenged me to be aware of the emotional carrying capacity in my children; how much can they bear without it stunting them in some way? That's no doubt something you do on a case-by-case basis while also taking into account the personality differences between your children. It's difficult work, but they're worth it. As we try and figure it out I'd like to offer this suggestion, per my girls: stay close, lock arms, and hold hands, fingers and all.

> Become a student of your children;
> try and learn their emotional carrying
> capacity, as well as your own.

IN WEAKNESS

God had a son he loved.

I have a son I love.

God watched the sorrow and the nails.

I would not wish it but I believe I could bear it too;

I understand the pride of pain.

But God never had a daughter. If so

he could not have borne her passion.

I say this for I have two daughters.

I confess there are days

I love them more than

I love God, or at least more

than I love truth.

So yes, in weakness I love them.

But I am the father of girls.

FIVE

LISTENING AND SILENCE

✦✦✦✦✦✦✦✦✦

When the righteous cry out, the Lord listens;
he delivers them from all their troubles.

—Psalm 34:17

OUR YOUNGEST DAUGHTER began vomiting Monday morning around 8 o'clock. At 8 P.M., she was still vomiting, unable to keep anything down. We debated between taking her to the ER and trying to ride out the night, hoping it would stop. We prayed and opted to wait and see if things got better. We went to bed and nothing stopped; in fact, it seemed to grow worse. Probably twice an hour, every hour, my four-year-old little girl would begin to cough up evil itself; we'd sit her up, and her body would heave in painful contractions until the episode would fade.

We had been praying for her all day long and had amped up our efforts when night fell. I'm not sure where you fall on the prayer spectrum, if at all. My wife and I were raised in a tradition of prayer and we have chosen to continue it. We do this not because we have to (out of duty) but because we have to (life is hard and we are weak). So we pray, but ours are not elaborate table-cloth prayers, they never have been. In this specific situation they were usually along the lines of "God, c'mon, make the vomiting stop" or "Give it to me, pass it over to my stomach and my throat and my lungs. She's too little." We prayed phrases like these at least twice an hour, every hour, all night long.

And nothing changed. No deliverance, no nothing.

We took her to the hospital the next morning and sure enough, she was severely dehydrated and required an overnight stay and several bags of IV fluid. I confess I was not on speaking terms with God that morning. I further confess I don't believe such behavior on my part throws God into some tizzy. If it did I would cease to pray; the last thing I need is a deity easily unsettled.

My wife stayed with Abbey that first day and I came the next for my shift. I sat in what the hospital calls a "chair" and read while Abbey slept and a clear tube refilled her tanks. I was reading Frederick Buechner wax on about listening to your life, and how if you want to hear God speaking you should listen to your life and what's going on and what you're feeling or thinking or doing. I thought, "OK, Fred. Fine. Here we go." I listened to the life I had lived the past forty-eight hours. I listened and watched while the tears of a mother ran down her cheeks like fast rain. I listened and heard the quiet of my youngest daughter who normally has no use for anything related to silence. I listened and felt the one eye open/one eye shut mode of sleeping that we had participated in all night long. I listened and saw a brother and sister hold back their sister's long auburn hair as her body heaved.

And in all that listening, I started hearing voices in my head:

Well, maybe you weren't praying hard enough?

Hard enough? You're kidding, right? We knocked on heaven's door until our knuckles bled.

Well, maybe there's junk in your own
life clogging the lines and
you need to take care of that first?

What, so God won't move unless the lines are clear? If that were the prerequisite, nothing would ever happen.

Well, maybe it was a test.
God won't put more on you than you can handle, you know.

It sure didn't look like Abbey was able to handle it; in fact, it seemed to handle her. And am I to believe that God would allow pain to visit her in order to teach me some lesson?

Well, I'm sure someone, somewhere was suffering more.

You know, I can't tell you how crummy that sentence sounds. You can only play the people-are-starving-in-China-so-eat-your-beans card so many times; eventually the bluff gets called. When my daughter was vomiting her head off the other night, I never once thought, *hmm, well at least this isn't the Holocaust or 9/11 or . . .*

It must've been God's will.

Please, don't get me started. It's hard to pinpoint the headwaters of this voice, but it completely sounds like well-meaning Christians over the years who don't know what else to say in the face of suffering. I get it, I've said it too. It sounds good but a slight scratch beneath the surface and you come face-to-face with resignation. I have found that sometimes, in the face of suffering, it is best to say nothing, nothing at all.

Why do bad vomiting episodes happen to good little four-year-olds? I don't know. I'm open to the response that Jesus' disciples got when they asked him why a man was born blind: "so that God's mighty works might be displayed" (John 9:3). But if I recall the story correctly, the blind man received his sight. He got what he needed. Me, I'm still blind, not knowing what the hell went on those few days. We asked for bread and felt like we got stones and serpents. The world is a cruel place. This much we know.

After a couple of rehydrating days we brought Abbey home, to her room and her bed and her toys and her dog. I kept chewing on Buechner's challenge: listen to your life.

Here's what I think I heard: *You made it*. I didn't find that satisfying at all, but that's what I think I heard. And I've heard it on more than one such occasion in my days of fathering.

Some days or weeks or years don't make a lick of sense, or at least we can't make heads or tails of them. And the prayers we pray in those seasons may go unanswered, at least as far as we can tell. But maybe God is silent in those moments because sometimes in the face of suffering it is best to say nothing at all. It has nothing to do with weakness but everything to do with respect.

Some days there's no help, just trouble upon trouble. On days like that listen to your life. It may be all you can do.

SIX

MAKING SPACE FOR SAD

✦✦✦✦✦✦✦✦✦

We are preoccupied with time. If we could
learn to love space as deeply as we are now
obsessed with time, we might discover a new
meaning in the phrase to live like men.

—*Edward Abbey*

JUST BEFORE THE THANKSGIVING break, my son's
best friend moved away. His dad got a job out East, so their
family loaded up the truck and moved to Kentucky. My son
watched them drive away. Those boys have been good friends

for over a year now. They were both in the accelerated classes at school, so the friendship was born from a competitive root. Brandon would often come over to our house after school and I'd walk by Will's room and hear them arguing like an old married couple. Neither wanted to give in or admit defeat; crying uncle was out of the question.

The first few times I heard them one-upping, I stepped in and told them to be "nice." Yeah, that was a dad-strike-out; they looked at me like a calf looks at a new gate. What I learned was that was the way they communicated with each other: competitive, bristly, sparks flying, alive.

Will's had a hard time this week. We didn't really know what was going on, he's just been moody and easily upset (redundant, I know). Last night we were working on multiplication tables and there was a problem he didn't remember how to do. I asked if he listened to the teacher that day. "Yes, Dad." I asked if somebody was talking and he couldn't hear. "No, Dad." I asked if he couldn't see the board for some reason. "I could see it fine, Dad." I asked if the person sitting next to him was bothering him or cracking jokes. "I was sitting by myself, Dad." Oh. Bingo.

Grief just does weird things to you. Your best friend moves away and all of a sudden, you're alone. The guy who sat beside you for over a year at school is not in his chair anymore; a vacancy exists in that room you call your own. The friend you competed with in EVERYTHING finally gave up and had to go with his family. He conceded and you still lost. That's hard enough for me to stomach let alone a nine-year-old boy. My son is grieving and man, it's hard to watch. I can't bring Brandon back. I can't arrange for a new friend to emerge to take his place.

We walk through a vale of tears on this earth and the only way through it is through it. It is a lesson we learn and live. We accept it and gradually realize our part in the pain; if we didn't care, it wouldn't hurt. But all this can make us stumble and bumble and forget how to do partial product multiplication problems and it causes us to sit by ourselves and be moody and easily upset and redundant. And sad.

Patty Loveless sings a beautiful country song that goes something like this:

> How can I help you to say goodbye?
> It's OK to hurt, and it's OK to cry.

I believe it's OK to be sad; in other words, there ought to be space in our lives to learn the texture of sadness. So that's what my wife and I did, we gave Will some space. We didn't abandon him but we gave him some room, and there's a difference. He's beginning to experience the ache that comes with caring for others. And although he couldn't articulate it, I believe he's sensing that *closure* is a fool's word.

When they need it, give your kids the gift of space. Trust they're learning something. Chances are good they are.

SEVEN

TIME OUT #1

✦✦✦✦✦✦✦✦✦

From TIME TO TIME we've tried putting our kids in time out. It's never been effective for them, but it has given us, the parents, a chance to catch a breath. We were able to realize that, yes, this too will pass (fingers crossed).

Consider this a brief time out, after several stories, to iterate what this is all about. Fatherhood is a gamble. You can call it a risk, an adventure, the game, a challenge, whatever you want, but at the heart of it all is a continual rolling of the dice and not knowing what's going to happen. Can you ensure certain outcomes with your kids? Yes, if you force it you absolutely can. And odds are they'll hate you for it. Oh, they might forgive you one of these days and you can all have a hugfest at the bitter end, but for most of their days they'll hate you. And you'll hate yourself, if not openly then secretly.

I'm not sure how many people still recite the old vows in their marriage ceremonies. There are always variations but these lines form the heart—

> to have and to hold from this day forward,
>
> for better or for worse,
>
> for richer, for poorer,
>
> in sickness and in health,
>
> to love and to cherish,
>
> 'til death do us part.

The thing is, you speak those words and you have no idea what's to come with your spouse; those phrases cover a multitude of experiences—it's like rolling dice. It's the same with kids. In fact, fathering vows wouldn't be a bad idea at the outset, pledging to have and to hold sons and daughters in the full sturm and drang of your lives together, in a very real way 'til death parts you.

I know some consider Kenny Rogers's "The Gambler" to be a cheesy song. Maybe it is. But do you recall those phrases about *know when to hold 'em* and *fold 'em*? *Know when to walk away* and *when to run*? Those are fathering gold. They don't make fatherhood easier necessarily but that perspective provides a little sanity "'til death parts you" or as Kenny sings 'til *the dealing's done*. Fatherhood is all about learning.

Oh, and don't forget—you have to play the hand (kids) you're dealt.

EIGHT

MAKING THE CUT

✦✦✦✦✦✦✦✦✦

. . . that what is called for is not subjugation but genuflection.

—Barry Lopez

JUST FOUR WEEKS AGO. Just four weeks ago they were knee-deep in summer. Today they start back to school. Big kids. That's what I've got. No longer do they drink from sippy cups or sit in a car seat or watch *Clifford*. Well, sometimes they still watch the big red dog. Now they listen to Hannah Montana and play GameCube and laugh at adult humor. Too fast, too soon. They may be ready for this day, but I'm certain I'm not. Then again I'm partly to blame.

The doctor let me cut the umbilical cord on all our kids. I released them into this world. William Blake has words that rang in my head as I made the cut: "My mother groaned, my father wept: / Into the dangerous world I leapt." I wouldn't trade that experience for anything and I always encourage expectant fathers to do the same.

I'm planning to go in to work late this morning; my cutting skills are needed again. My children need to be released from the warm womb of summer, set free into the rhythm of the school year. Their mother will groan. It feels harder this year because our youngest starts kindergarten. She's the last one.

I'm not sure if that lump under my breastbone will rise there on the playground or not. If it does, it does. They will be leaping into the dangerous world yet again and I want to be there when they jump. Because I'm partly to blame.

Is it a wonderful life? You bet. But is it a dangerous world? Yes, it is. We still sit cross-legged in the floor and play Uno, but there are registered sex offenders in our area. We still kiss and hug everybody before bed, do the tickle monster some nights too. But there are also men and women dying daily in Iraq and Old Navy blue jean commercials that have nothing to do with blue jeans. They'll spend recess on the swings many days, but they'll have friends who think they're too big to swing and want to do other things during recess.

O God of backpacks and lockers and new shoes and first days of school, please keep my children this day. They are leaping into it once again. I believe you go before them

in all things, from language skills to lunch. It is a dangerous world you've created, God, but it's also so beautiful.
Maybe you felt this way when Adam and Eve leapt into
the land east of Eden—your kids, going off to school. As
you stood there, hands blood-wet from cutting them loose,
I wonder if you wept? I wonder if you felt partly to blame?
I know I do. Amen.

It is a wonderful life. It is a dangerous world.
We cannot have one without the other.
Of the lessons we must teach our
children, this is surely on the list.

COMMON TRIBE

I once read that as bitter March winds
blew Crazy Horse cradled his daughter's
still body in his arms and lay down with
her on a small burial platform as she died
from the white man's cough. She was called
They Are Afraid of Her, his only daughter.
As this greatest of all Sioux men held her
tightly in a red blanket, the wolves sang a
beautiful chorus and she was lifted into a
better heaven than our own. I am not a
Sioux chief but I am a father so I believe
he tried to summon her back to life as Jesus
did to Lazarus, but found he was too late.
I read further that ravens black as pitch
began to circle overhead the lifeless red
bundle as Crazy Horse rode away hard
with tears loosened by the cold wind that
blew the colder stars around the sky.
Then, as a father, I became so lost in my
own visions I simply could read no more.

NINE

WHAT A BOY NEEDS

✦✦✦✦✦✦✦✦✦

stay together

learn the flowers

go light

—*Gary Snyder*

I CAME HOME YESTERDAY to find my son and a friend standing around their bicycles, talking and passing something between their hands. For what reason I don't know, but lines from Gary Snyder popped up in the junkyard of my mind. The boys saw me and hopped on their bikes (*stay together*) and rode down to the end of our street, a cul-de-sac, then off their bikes and up a lonely pine that grows there. I could see their feet scrambling up the low, squatty branches until they found a roosting spot (*learn the flowers*). There they sat and talked.

I went inside and my wife and I prepared dinner. "Why don't you go call the boys in." "OK," I said. I walked to the edge of the driveway and gave my best dad-to-son-call: "Will, come home." The boys heard me, scrambled down the tree, mounted their bikes, and rode home. As they dismounted, I noticed pocket knives in their hands (*go light*).

He told me later (*stay together*) that they were talking, looking at their knives, hanging out in the tree. They also found a bottle of vodka with a little left in the bottom. "You guys oughta stay away from that stuff." "Sure, Dad. We threw the bottle down the hill" (*learn the flowers*).

For now I am thankful for my son and his friends and their bikes and that pine tree with low branches and those pocket knives. And for vodka bottles that were thrown away, for now (*go light*).

We must learn what it takes to have
an ongoing relationship with our children:
stay . . . learn . . . go.

TEN

THE NEEDS OF THE MANY

✦✦✦✦✦✦✦✦✦

Where there's desolation and heartbreak . . .
there's beauty and magic.

—*Harry Middleton*

RECENTLY MY BROTHER AND his family made the
pilgrimage from Texas out to Colorado to visit us. We spent
a few days around town and then headed for the mountains.
Grand Lake, to be specific. There's really not any other option
than to be happy when you're in Grand Lake, Colorado, for the
week with your family and your brother and his.

I remember all of us squeezing into one vehicle (four adults, five kids) just before dusk and heading out to see if we could spot a moose. We weaved the mountain roads snug as bugs in a rug. Our hopes of seeing a moose never came to pass, but on the way back into town one of the kids did get carsick and proceeded to do what kids do when they get carsick.

I had happened to throw my ultra-cool Patagonia running top in the car before we left. It was the closest thing to my wife when the hurling started, so in order to keep the interior of my brother's SUV driveable, she grabbed my shirt and saved the evening. Was I a little sad about the shirt? Sure, I really looked good in it and I felt it made me more swift. But sometimes the needs of the many outweigh the needs of the few, or the dad.

After we got back to the cabin, I spent the rest of the evening running, as in running my ultra-cool top through the washing machine. With each rinse cycle a little more of my sadness was rinsed away as well until the point that the whole thing was comical. I lost a good shirt but we made a memory still laughed about to this day. Everybody got a big kick out of it, finally even me. In fact, my brother and I laughed about it until we cried. I'll gladly trade running a little less uber-cool for the memory of my only brother and me laughing like boys on a high altitude porch as night crept over a very grand lake while aspens quaked nearby. I'm sure there were moose just beyond our sight.

Maybe when our kids are older they'll decide to get together for the summer with their cousins. Maybe they'll sit on a porch somewhere, maybe in the mountains, and they'll say, "Hey, do you remember Uncle John's pretty-boy running shirt getting hosed that night in Grand Lake?" And my youngest will say, "Yeah, I did it!" Then they'll all laugh until they get a little misty and say, "Man, that's a great memory. Didn't we have a good time?" And they'll all say, "Yeah, we really did."

By that time I'll probably be in assisted living quarters or something, possibly sitting in a wheelchair out on a screened-in-porch with photographs of mountains on the wall. Maybe my mind will be all but gone. But at the exact moment when those beautiful grown children on a porch in the mountains say, "Yeah, we really did," there will be a quaking of the aspen tree planted in my heart and memory will be stirred across the miles and the old man in the wheelchair that I may be will stand and face the western skies and whisper out in the voice of a witness: "Yes, it was a grand time. I was there. I remember." Chances are good if that happens some cute twenty-year-old assisting nurse will walk by and say, "Mr. Blase, sit back down now. Everything's OK." And I'll defiantly refuse and keep standing, if just for a little while. Standing for me. Standing for my dear brother. Standing for our gentle wives. Standing for our brave children. Standing for a running shirt's early demise. Standing for the moose still shrouded in mist. Standing in gratitude because I do remember. That nurse will probably walk up to me, take my hand and say, "Your wife has had her bath.

She's waiting for you back in your room." And I'll sit in the chair as she rolls me back to my room. I'd like to roll myself, but I may not remember the way.

Sometimes the needs of the many
outweigh the needs of the dad.
And sometimes those are the
best times.

ELEVEN

A DIFFERENT ROAD

✦✦✦✦✦✦✦✦✦

Beware, O wanderer, the road is walking too.

—*Rainer Maria Rilke*

WE WERE SITTING AROUND the dinner table the other night when one of our kids said something about someone named "Samson." Being the engaged father I seldom am but dream of being, I quickly asked in follow-up, hoping to cue a Bible learning moment, "And who else do you know named Samson?" Our middle daughter responded, "Samson was the name of the dog in that movie." It was said matter-of-factly, her siblings seemed to agree, and the conversation moved on to other topics. My wife and I just looked at each other. "Baby, we gotta do something."

We are the parents who have gently moved away from structures such as Sunday school, Vacation Bible School, and those after-school-memorize-a-kazillion-verses-so-you-can-put-patches-on-your-vest programs. We haven't abandoned our faith, given up on God, or written off sermons; well, the jury's still out on sermons. But we have stopped to think about all the curriculum we grew up with, and while at the stop sign we've wondered if we want our children to grow up in the same fashion.

We want our children to have a vibrant faith measured by heart love more than head knowledge. We do realize they go together but we do want them to get the heart before the course. We've been in too many B-Christian subculture movies where someone quotes chapter and verse blindfolded and then turns around and does something completely opposed to what they just quoted.

But how do parents like us pass along a biblical literacy to their children without it becoming rote memorization? Even more, how do we help them hide a sacred text in their hearts but not so well that they can't remember where they put it? How can I introduce my daughter to Samson before he was a dog?

I'm not wringing my hands in some Chicken-Little-the-sky-is-falling-because-my-kids-don't-know-who-Samson-is moment. We pray at mealtimes and other moments when prayer feels right. I remember praying with one of the kids when they were constipated—"Lord, help me go"—and that prayer was just as natural as breathing for them. Look, if we can't ask the Lord for help when we're blocked up, then we're really in trouble.

Yet I still want them to know of Samson and David and Peter, Paul, and Mary. Of Adam and his pretty wife Eve, and Noah—the man who bought a zoo. Of Nathan and the healing waters of Siloam. Of young Timothy and his upset stomach. Of Elizabeth whose womb leapt with John the Baptist. Of Joseph who did the right thing and married the girl God got pregnant. These are good people who have been friends for my journey. And then of course there's Jesus, the Lamb of God, who took away the sins of the world.

Well, John, the voice inside my head once more surfaces, *you realize that you know all those people because you rotely memorized verses and attended VBS all those years and sat under faithful Sunday school teachers every Sunday, don't you?*

Yes, I do. And I believe all those things prepared me for this time and these kids. But our children are growing up along a different track of faith; same God, different road—a road littered with dogs named Samson.

You can't raise your kids exactly like you were raised.
Besides, you don't want them to
turn out exactly like you anyway.

TWELVE

THANKSGIVING

✦✦✦✦✦✦✦✦✦

God is great, God is good.

Let us thank him for this food.

SOME FOLKS SAY WE ARE a people obsessed with food. Maybe. I say that we are a people obsessed with communion, we just don't always know how to get there. We love each other so much it hurts, it really does, but we don't know how to approach one another. So when we can, we wash our hands and don our aprons and crack open the good books and de-lid the cans of broth and step into a hoped-for grace.

Going back home is always hard. You got married, moved away, spread your wings a little, had kids, grew a ponytail—the typical arc of leaving home. Holidays roll around and at least for some of us there's the pull, the tractor beam on the chromosomal level that says "Hey, go see your family why don'tcha? What, don'tcha love 'em?" And so you do, knowing that it's never like you build it up in your mind to be. You know the drill: the first day back is jubilant, then the next day is filled with tending to things, and by the third day a vague unrest often settles in. But one of these days you'll want your kids to come visit on Thanksgiving, so you do it.

The thing is, while you flew the coop the rest of your family members didn't just sit around waiting for your return; they spread their wings too just maybe not as wide. In other words, even though things do stay the same they also change; so returning home is often like stepping into a conversation that's already going on. All that to say thank God for food; it's a vehicle for our desires to commune with people we care about, and if our holidays sometimes revolve completely around food, that makes perfect sense. Get over it.

For example, I watched as my daughter and my mom followed recipes together and found their hands in the common ground of chocolate, rising flour, fruit, and salad. All the other conversations the two of them had going on in their heads had to be put on hold, if even for just a little while, as attention was paid to measuring correctly, greasing where appropriate, and preheating like Paula Deen says. My daughter and my mom communed with one another in those moments; it was beautiful to see.

I also saw my wife, her sister, and their mother all focused on what actually goes in the dressing. All other thoughts, important as they might be, were paused as celery, sage, cornbread, eggs, onions (I have to stop there or I'll give away their secrets) were chopped, grated, torn asunder, and lightly beaten. These three ladies moved around one another in this culinary dance, this kitchen shuffle leading right up to communion. Being in one another's lives after not being in one another's lives for weeks or months at a time made possible by food.

At my parents' I was given the honor of cutting the bird for the table. You must know Norman Rockwell would not have chosen me as his carving model, so this is not really an honor as much as fodder for after-dinner wisecracks. Not always, but this time around I was able to set that pressure aside and proceed to strip the bird, quickly abandoning the knife in favor of the hands. And for a few moments I was quiet, standing there pulling away the meat to put on a platter so my family could come by and pile their plates high. They did and in those moments we were all together. My daughters prefer white meat, my dad has always been a leg man, and I've always had a penchant for dark meat. I felt priestly, handing out this alternative bread; and with each piece placed just so on a relative's plate, I smile a smile that says, "I love you. I miss you. I'm glad to be here. Thanks for going to all the trouble. This'll probably get crazy by tonight and chances are good we'll head home earlier than planned, and while that may not be great, right now this is good."

It's transubstantiation, really, as one substance (food) changes into another (love). I believe in it. I've seen it happen.

"Man does not live by bread alone"
means there are other things
besides bread, but the bread's still important.

THIRTEEN

THE FATHER DREAM

✦✦✦✦✦✦✦✦✦

How can anyone be a father?

—*Kent Meyers*

OF THE SONGS THAT Judy Collins sings, my favorite is "My Father." The lyrics tell how her father always promised them that they *would live in France* where she *would learn to dance*. The reality was quite different; her father was blind and supported his family by working in radio. Still, the song indicates, her father's dreams more than kept their family alive; those dreams instilled in Collins and her sisters the belief that life was indeed a wonderful thing.

I have trouble making it through that song without tears. I have dreams for my children too. Some of those dreams I can make come true, some of them I can't, at least not right now. I would love for my girls to study under a great dance instructor, for my son to be able to attend that top-drawer football camp in the summer, for them to all have a room of their own, for there to be frequent trips to the mountains to ski or snowboard or just sit in a lodge by a fire nursing hot cocoa. Those aren't the only dreams I have for them, but they're some of them.

Are those dreams based on my children's dreams and desires? Yes, they are. Are some of them based on my own dreams? Sure, mine get mixed up in there as well. I wouldn't say mine have to do with specifics like dance or football, but more that broader dream, what I call "the father dream"—the one that says: "Go farther than me. I'll help you all I can."

I wonder what God's dreams are for us? Maybe they are as varied as our faces. Maybe God dreams that some of us will go boating on the Seine, or write screenplays, or play professional baseball, or go to cooking school, or teach children to read, or stand in a river hoping a fish will rise, or publish a book of poetry, or climb Pikes Peak, or pass the GED, or pay the heating bill, or stay married, or have their own room, or have someone to tuck them in and kiss them goodnight.

Or maybe God's dream is not so much specific as general; it's the Father dream—"Go far. I'll help you all I can." If that were true, and there has to be a smidgen of a possibility that it is, then think how swallowing that reality might change things. We might give love a second chance or even a third. We might do one more rewrite, even though we were exhausted. We might dust off the *whatever* and refuse to let some thief steal our dream. We might begin to believe that even with all the damnable struggles in life, that life is indeed a wonderful thing. And if we believe that, then maybe our children will too.

> Let your children hear your dreams.
> It is the way they learn to go farther.

FOURTEEN

MY FATHER'S GIFT

++++++++++

After six decades I've only recently understood
the degree to which I'm my father's son.

—*Jim Harrison*

I WAS HEADED OUT to shovel snow this morning.
Grabbed my jacket and gloves, sidestepped the Beagle, and
headed for the backdoor. Just before opening the door, I stuck
my hand in one of my black gloves. Suddenly I was a boy
again, trying on my father's black gloves for size, feeling their
volume and plush. And I found myself lost in memory.

My father is probably unaware of the times I pulled open the drawer that kept his things: T-shirts, cuff links, old watches. One of those items was a pair of gloves, probably refreshed by new pairs over the years, but they always seemed to be black. One pair in particular had a luxurious inner lining. I loved putting them on, stretching my fingers wide in their warmth.

My father now lives in Arkansas. I live in Colorado. I miss my dad being close-by today. I'm in a season of feeling rather boyish, small and of little account, overwhelmed, as the psalmist would say, by "matters too great for me." I'm longing for that strength my dad always brought to our house. I can only remember fear on the days or nights when he was away. And that wasn't very often. But when his presence wasn't there, the fear was palpable.

Presence. I realize it's a counterintuitive idea for most parents these days but I'd like to suggest that simply being there is as important as what you do when you're there. The cultural pressure to be this fully engaged father reminds me of that picture of Atlas carrying the world on his shoulders; that's a little much, don'tcha think? Maybe one of the primary roles of the father in a child's life is to be there, on-site, in the scene, to keep the fear at bay. Not to interfere, but to protect simply by presence.

I read the following passage from a D. H. Lawrence essay, *Education of the People,* published in 1918: "How to begin to educate a child. First rule: leave him alone. Second rule: leave him alone. Third rule: leave him alone. That is the whole beginning." This kind of thinking can obviously lead to careless parenting, but it doesn't have to. It can have a carefree nature to it, and what a beautiful gift to a son or daughter, seeing a lightness in a father when too often our children see weariness.

We sons are too harsh on our fathers; I know I was back in my early thirties. *Why didn't we do this?* or *why didn't you teach me that?* Those are fair questions, but I'm not sure they're just. Are there fathers out there completely oblivious to their children and what their children need? No question. But there are also as many fathers out there who are giving their children the gift of presence, keeping the fear away. After four decades I'm only recently beginning to understand this, this gift that I am able to give my children because it was first given to me by my father. There were plenty of verbal affirmations and hugs along the way, but the sterling thing is that he was there. I'm just now beginning to see that.

I'd like to believe my father was aware of the times I got into his things, that he made sure cuff links were there to be found and handled. And luxurious black gloves were there to be tried on for size.

I've no doubt my neighbor looked out the window this morning and said, "Honey, John is just standing there again, leaning on the snow shovel. Should I go help him or something?" And my neighbor probably answered his own question. "No. He does that from time to time. He'll be OK."

It's strange. A forty-year old man sticks a hand in a glove and is suddenly ten years old again, trying out his father's things. It's a profound truth that simple items become relics of something sacred when memory is involved. And what is that sacred thing? The presence in our lives of those who love us. They didn't have to be there, but they were. We are called to a life of genuflection, something you can do with gloves on, or off.

Don't leave them lonely,
but leave your children alone.
Your presence is the gift they'll later cherish.

GLEANERS

If he knows the grandkids are coming

he leaves piles of quarters and

nickels and dimes on his nightstand,

along with a few starlight mints.

He's been doing this for years now.

He knows they never ask,

just take, all they can get.

He gets joy out of it,

them getting away with something of his.

It's his way of giving them a tie

to bind, later, after he's gone.

Remember when we used to steal Papa's change?

And maybe, just maybe,

they will in turn love the small and poor

as they were loved.

FIFTEEN

THE VOW

❖❖❖❖❖❖❖❖❖

Expose a child to a particular environment
at his susceptible time
and he will perceive in the shapes
of that environment until he dies.

—*Wallace Stegner*

THERE IS A BLACK-AND-WHITE photograph that sits in my parents' kitchen. My dad pointed it out again to me recently, saying, "That's my favorite picture of your mom and me." It was taken on the steps of a chapel, not long after my parents were married. It basically shows a couple of kids in love. Skinny, smiling, arms around the other's waist, and wide-eyed. After that photo was taken, they walked down those steps into the rest of their lives.

I don't know all the reasons why that's my dad's favorite photograph. I don't need to know. But when I look into it I see two people with the promise of things to come before them, the vast sea of possibilities. My father became a preacher. My mother became a schoolteacher. She taught high school math, so I was never in her classroom. But nevertheless she taught me many things. If I were pressed to name two things my mother taught me, I'd have to say 1) to iron a shirt. Some of my best ideas come while I'm ironing my shirts, plus I don't pay a dry cleaner to do something I can do myself.

And 2) Mom ends our conversations with "I love you." She has always done that. I'd like to think that was a vow she made back on those black-and-white steps many years ago: "I will love this life and all that it brings me." That is a lesson I learned from her and I pray my children learn from me. As for teaching my kids to iron, let's not hold our breath.

"I will love this life and all that it brings me."
This is the vow you must make each day.

SIXTEEN

BUT SOMETIMES

✦✦✦✦✦✦✦✦✦

Do not believe that he who seeks to comfort
you lives untroubled among the simple and
quiet words that sometimes do you good.
His life has much difficulty and sadness . . .
Were it otherwise he would never have been
able to find those words.

—*Rainer Maria Rilke*

BUT SOMETIMES THERE are moments when everything seems right.

I came home last night to a warm house, in more ways than one. We held hands and voiced a prayer before beginning our meal. We didn't ask for anything, just simply said "thank you." We all sat at our table for five and ate ham and cheese sandwiches accompanied by cracked salt-n-pepper potato chips. Everyone ate what was in front of them; it was almost in the realm of the miraculous. Our youngest said, "Mom, this is a recipe you have to give us when we have our own families." My, my. The recipe for ham and cheese sandwiches. It must indeed be the little things.

We talked all at once, what the kids had done that day, they asked me about my workday, we finished off the bag of chips. We talked about some dreams and it was fun dreaming. Somebody said they were going to live in Paris (ugh, figures). Somebody else is going to live in Indiana since he'll be a professional football player (he says they make good money). And the littlest piggie said she was going to live close to mom and dad, visiting quite often, her and her husband and kids and their dog. My hope is she'll bring ham and cheese sandwiches. I hope all of our dreams come true.

Dinner was ended when the dog threw up four times. Somebody might as well have pulled the pin on a grenade. Nothing like a yarking Beagle to hasten the phrase, "You're excused." We got everything cleaned up; actually, I cleaned up the floor. A father's bravery is called forth in interesting ways in the burbs.

We received Yahtzee for Christmas and so we decided to play a round or two. Everyone can play Yahtzee, even our five-year-old. Rolling dice and shouting phrases like "full house" and "large straight" is intoxicating. It made us feel like river-boat gamblers. We played until the scores were to be tallied. I was "off" last night, coming in fourth out of five. My wife said, "That's OK. I still love you." Words and phrases like that make a man clean up Beagle barf without hesitation.

We listened to some Christmas music (in September) while Yahtzee-ing. Somebody asked, "Why are we listening to this?" Somebody else said, "Because Dad wants to, and he did clean up the mess." The music was quiet, piano solos mostly, not exactly riverboat music, but it seemed the perfect musi-cal backdrop for our table-round. Interspersed between "three of a kind" and "what's that smell?" were the strains of "Silent Night" and "What Child Is This?"

The two logicians in our family tallied their scores and kept playing a personal dice-off of some kind. The remaining three non-logicians, myself included in that number, looked around for some cookies. We eventually all got up from the gambling table and went to do other things, things like put-ting dishes in the dishwasher, sliding down the stairs in an old sleeping bag; you know, normal riverboat doings. The piano winterlude music ended and that place deep within my bones wished it would not. *Dear God, can't the music last a little longer? Please?* But it did not. The dice were put away and the dancing girls went to bed. One dancing boy too. And a dancing, fully recovered Beagle.

And my wife in her kerchief and I in my cap settled down to read a little. A night like that may not happen again for weeks or months. My fingers are crossed it doesn't take that long, but I know it might. Such is the life of riverboat gamblers and daughters who want to live in Paris and weak-stomached dogs and non-logician fathers like me. And the little girl who is going to live close to mom and dad.

There are moments of much difficulty. But there are also moments when everything seems right. *Carpe momentum*.

Seize the moments when they happen.
Then let them pass.
Others will come, but it may be a while.

SEVENTEEN

FULLY NAKED,
ALMOST ASHAMED

✦✦✦✦✦✦✦✦✦

Stories bind us by reminding us that our lives
all exhibit the same fragilities,
and thus demand that we stay humane.

—*William Kittredge*

IN THE EIGHTH GRADE I was the skinny, trumpet-
playing band guy who signed up for off-season weight lifting. My schedule, for some reason, afforded that flexibility,
so I wanted to take advantage of it. Most of my friends were

not-so-skinny football or basketball players and I desired to be more like them. With the exception of some Little League baseball, I had not participated in any organized sports.

On the first day of off-season, coaches handed us cleats, shorts, T-shirt, socks, and a jockstrap. We then filed into a dressing room to suit up. I knew of cleats and shorts and T-shirts and socks, but this jock piece stumped me. No one had prepared me for it; we didn't have anything like that in the trumpet section. It looked like someone had gotten really creative with a pair of scissors and come up with a down-sized pair of underwear. From what I could gather, however, no one else around me seemed to have a problem with this piece of equipment. It was one of those moments of being completely surrounded by others yet feeling totally alone.

I undressed and picked up this strange foundational piece. I would so like to tell you a different story here; this one is so fragile. But I feel I must tell you the truth. I stuck my feet in the straps and started pulling the jockstrap up—*backwards*. I quickly had all the support I could possibly stand in a region that needed no help. Meanwhile, my skinny eighth-grade male anatomy was about to face the world of weights and coaches and wind sprints with no protection. Metaphor, anyone?

A large, dark figure stepped in front of me as I pulled this elasticized potentiality of shame slowly up my legs. He was buck naked and had all the trappings of a full-grown man. Our eyes met, he grinned then humanely said, "Other way, man," and then walked away. At that point in my life I'd never seen a picture of a black angel, but from that moment on I believed in their existence; I'd had a visitation. I sat down on that cold dressing room bench and slowly untangled my feet from the straps. My movements were slow with the weight of shame and embarrassment and gratitude. Was I just supposed to know this? My junior high boyish mind guessed so. I made a vow that day to never be caught again not knowing the worldly ways of men. I started reading *Esquire* magazine not long after that, not exactly the best resource for manly things, but it was something.

I believe my father could have prepared me for that moment, I really do. He just probably didn't think about it. I have missed such moments in the lives of my children, just not thinking or, worse, thinking about something else totally unrelated to what my children may be going through. It is a part of the pain in a father's heart, knowing you can't remember everything and in those gaps of not-thinking sometimes your children slip and fall into shame-filled places. I suppose mothers experience this same pain in a mother's way. It's overwhelming, this knowledge that you can't keep your children from moments like that. But you also know, as hard as it is to know such things, that there are times when your sons and daughters have to step into something with their own two feet. Sometimes that's something as simple as a jockstrap, other times it's not so simple.

And that is at least one reason I hold fast to a God surrounded by angels dispensed to come to our aid, sentinels with messages like *Other way, man.*

Sometimes your sons and
daughters have to step
into something with their own two feet.

EIGHTEEN

LUCKY ONES

✦✦✦✦✦✦✦✦✦

Judging it now, I believe what
I felt most was gratitude.

—*Ivan Doig*

HER NAME IS ABBEY. She is my youngest gift from
the Grace that keeps this world. She's six years old and has
recently experienced a row of freckle-seeds blossom under
both her eyes. On Saturday, around noon, she stated: *Dada,
I want you to play with me* in a clear, direct, and persuasive
tone. "OK," I said, and followed her back to the bedroom she

shares with her sister. Freckle-girl then told me that we were going to play birthday party (hers) and I was to be in charge of all the gifts (for her).

I asked her to write on her chalkboard what her desired gifts were; this would give Dada an idea of what to look for in the room of the birthday princess. She quickly wrote, south-paw that she is, ten items on the board.

As I began assembling the royal gifts, she handed me a little red box. Actually, it's a little red safe, complete with combination lock on the front so that big brother and middle sister cannot get into her things. She stated: *Dada, there's probably some stuff in here you can use.* I said "OK," and she opened it for me. Then she set about to other princessly administrivia.

I knew about the little red safe, but I hadn't seen it in a while, and it had been even longer since I'd seen any contents. This is what I found:

1. a piece of notebook paper folded like you would a letter, and written on it were several words in pencil

2. seven polished rocks that she bought with her money last summer in Grand Lake, Colorado

3. six Gameboy cartridges all lined up in a row

4. ten pieces of chalk, all broken, not a one whole and pristine

5. three hair clips

6. a dollar bill.

But this is what I *saw*:

1. a left-handed princess who knows she'll have to practice just a little harder at writing than her big brother and middle sister [the virtue of persistence]
2. stone reminders of a wonderful fairy-tale week with family and cousins in a cabin in the mountains by a gorgeous lake where every evening was accentuated by sugar cones at the ice cream store [memory muses]
3. quiet admiration for big brother and pride at being the sister upon whom his used video games fit like a glass slipper [what a poet calls "the arrogance of belonging"]
4. a strange comfortableness with things broken; in fact, an understanding that most things work better with the new rubbed off [the gift of grace]
5. an awareness that her Beagle will eat hair clips if they're not kept safe [the reality of danger]
6. gradual lessons in the power of money; what it can buy, like a bag of polished rocks [the reality of this life]

The ark of the covenant housed the tablets upon which God's finger wrote the commands for his people to follow. The Hebrew children regarded this box as containing the very power and presence of the Almighty. We all have our lesser-arks; places where we keep things sacred or holy to us, little red boxes full of the power and presence we bring to this world. And we do what we can to keep the contents safe, even using a combination lock if necessary. From time to time, we open these boxes and share their contents with the lucky ones.

There is a difference between what you see
and what is there.
This is very, very important.

NINETEEN

TODAY IS TODAY

✦✦✦✦✦✦✦✦✦

There are, however, small parts of every
human past that resist this natural cycle:
there are hard, cross-grained whorls of
memory that remain inexplicably lodged in
us long after the straight-grained narrative
material that housed them has washed away.
Most of these whorls are not stories, exactly:
more often they're self-contained moments
of shock or of inordinate empathy, moments
of violence, uncaught dishonesty, tomfoolery;
of mystical terror; lust; preposterous love;
preposterous joy.

—*David James Duncan*

MY SON "GRADUATES" today from elementary school. Sunrise, sunset. He'll be headed to middle school in the fall, the land of sixth- to eighth-graders and who knows what else.

My son, I am well pleased with you. It seems a breath ago that I took those scissors from Doc Brown's hand and cut you free from your mother. Only a breath. But one breath follows another, if we live, and today finds you standing on the shore, looking out at the sea of adolescence. You must know there are wonders to behold ahead. There are also waves and wind and storms. I believe that you have it within you to face what lies ahead. And I believe, as I believe you do, that there is One who goes before you. Always before you.

You entered a fun-run when you were six years old. Just as the race started, you got tripped-up and fell in a clump of boys. As you stood up your knee was bleeding; you began to cry. When you looked around you found my eyes, eyes that spoke *My son, I believe you can do this*. Then you amazed me by finishing the run, the entire one mile. I ran alongside you, cheering, hoping, praying. You finished the race bloodied and streaked with tears, and you stood with a medal around your neck. I believed on that day, as I do on this day, that your mother and I named you well.

Will - "strong, resolute one."

In what lies ahead I will still run beside you, as best I can, cheering, hoping, praying.

I could say much here about the days ahead. But today is today: still in the land of field trips and playgrounds and Saturdays where you don't have a care in the world. So, today, let's celebrate you. You have run well this first leg. I am well pleased with you, my first-born son. You bring me preposterous joy.

Children often grow into their names
if we'll only let them. Let them.

TWENTY

EVERYTHING TO HEART

✦✦✦✦✦✦✦✦✦

She said, "Glory, you take things too
much to heart." That was what they always
said about her. Hope was serene, Luke was
generous, Teddy was brilliant, Jack was
Jack, Grace was musical, and Glory took
everything to heart. She wished they had told
her how to do otherwise, what
else she should have done.

—*Marilynne Robinson*

MY SON RECEIVED a Wii gaming system for his birthday back in February. One of the aspects of the Wii that makes Nintendo people slaphappy but fathers and mothers not-so-slappy is the fact that most, if not all, of the games you purchase for this system cost thirty-five to fifty dollars. Whee!

He has his eyes on a particular game right now. He's played it at a friend's house. It's a decent game; I approve of it. So he approached me with a proposition, as is his custom: *Dad, if I read some books this summer that you choose, will you buy me that game?* I took his question to heart, as is my custom. *Sure. Let me think it over and I'll choose a couple of books. You'll have to give me an oral report after reading them though, OK?* His smile assured me the deal was sealed.

Now I'm stuck with the challenge of selecting books for him because he's already read so many; all the *Lord of the Rings, Harry Potter, Brian Jacques, Will Hobbs, Mike Lupica,* and all the Battle books on his school's reading list. I did an online search for reading lists appropriate to middle school (he starts in the fall). This was both encouraging and disappointing; he's read most all those books already. That makes me proud, but it turned what I thought would be an easy book pick into something harder, deeper, on the level of a quest.

I don't want to give him too much of a book to read, content-wise, and at the same time, I know how horrible it is to read a book that constantly insults your intelligence. And so I asked myself: *If I could encourage my son who often takes too much to heart, to read one book this summer, what would it be?* And it came to me.

Harper Lee's classic *To Kill a Mockingbird*. I handed him my copy and gave a brief character overview to get him started. I told him this was a book everyone needs to read but not everyone does. He said OK and immediately stepped into the story of Scout and Jem and Atticus and Dill and Boo.

I also told him that after he finishes, we'll watch the movie together one evening, bathe ourselves in black-and-white images accented by Leonard Bernstein's score. We'll watch Atticus shoot that rabid dog in the street and admire Scout's inherent scrap and hold our breath while old Bob Ewell spits in the face of Mr. Finch and feel sorry for Jem when he breaks his arm and be strangely drawn to a simple man named Boo Radley who stands in the shadows of a child's bedroom after saving the day.

Question: Are my son's motives mixed in this endeavor?

Answer: Sure. I don't care. Mine aren't.

C'mon. We're all about 7/10 bull-feathers anyway; we live mixed lives. If somebody's always banging the drum as to how pure their motives are, I'd suggest not spending a lot of time with them. It's like they're expending a lot of energy trying to convince not only you but themselves of something they're waffling on in the first place.

But as my son puts his hand to Miss Lee's plow with his sights set on harvesting a video game, my hope is that he will be swept away into the lives of those characters and take them too, too much to heart. His father experienced such a sweeping away years ago as Atticus became among the men he decided to model his life on.

The end doesn't always justify the means. But sometimes it does. As a father you have to make those decisions. That may mean standing in your child's shoes and walking around in them, maybe even getting swept away.

Take as much (too much even)
as you can to heart.
Get swept away. You won't regret it.

TWENTY-ONE

REPLACEMENT COSTS

✦✦✦✦✦✦✦✦✦

Life: another day, another dolor.

—*Edward Abbey*

MY WIFE HAD TO RUN an errand to The Dollar Store yesterday. The kids were with her, so as you might guess, the pleas began: *Come on, Mom, stuff's a dollar.* We're not rich, but on occasion we do have a few dollars. So all three offspring walked out of that high-quality establishment with something cheap.

Our youngest chose two plastic dolls: Strawberry Shortcake and Crepes Suzette. I'm not kidding, those are their real names. When I got home she was playing with them, took them with her into the bathtub, and only stopped the play later that evening when a Disney sitcom distracted her. In the few moments of taking her eyes and hands off of those two little smiling plastic girls, the Beagle decided to go cosmopolitan and try some Crepes Suzette. We heard him chewing over the sound of Disney characters wrestling with, of all things, friendship vs. popularity and when I pulled the doll from the dog and, well, let's just say now she is Crepes Su.

The cute little beret? Gone, gone. Those dainty little feet in espadrilles? Poof, vanished. There are ticks of time when, as a father, you know the dam's about to bust.

Our youngest busted—cried and screamed *I hate that dog!* The Beagle lowered his tail and eyes. I quickly asked if there were any more Crepes at The Dollar Store and her, *Yes, there are*, gave me enough gumption to promise to pick up another the next day to replace her current hatless, feetless doll. I do have to find a dollar, though.

Life's like that some days. You finally convince your mom to pony up with a George and you come home with two gloriously cheap toys and spend hours in Strawberryville. Turn your back for one minute and BAM! you're wrenched back to the reality of dogs who get bored and turn Crepes Suzettes into chew toys. You don't really hate the dog but it just feels like you can't get ahead.

Later that evening, I laid down to sleep praying, *Please let there be another Crepes Suzette on the rack. And please help me find a dollar.*

Some of the fathering job involves paying for
things you've already paid for once,
a.k.a., replacement costs.
If the original purchase came from The Dollar
Store, this is good thinking.

TWENTY-TWO

WAITING

✦✦✦✦✦✦✦✦✦

> . . . you can love completely without complete
> understanding.
>
> —*Norman Maclean*

AFTER THE ELEMENTARY school bell rang, my dad
would drive me out in the country to Mrs. Davis's house. She
taught me to play the piano. He took me, faithfully. I would
climb the steps to her house and sit under her instruction for
the forty-five minute lesson. And if memory serves, my dad
would sit and wait for me.

Waiting. It is one of the burdens of fathering.

I wonder now what he did while he waited. It seems he would sit in the car, a silver Renault wagon we had named "Betsy." I would sit with Mrs. Davis and play the scales and assigned pieces while my dad would sit with Betsy and possibly contemplate his upcoming sermon or pull out the latest copy of *Western Horseman* magazine and rehearse his secret life of being a cowboy.

I never quite understood what my father did while he was waiting. All I knew was that as I awkwardly descended the steps of the Davis house and re-entered my father's world, he was there. The door was always open.

We'd take the back way home and I'd often "drive" home, sitting in his lap. Hot, east Texas wind full of bird sound and crickets blew in the windows rolled down. Afternoons of tickling the ivories and navigating the ebony one-lane roads back home. And being with my dad.

Did my dad take me to piano lessons ten times, thirty times, seventy-five times? I don't know. It doesn't matter. Sometimes, a father doing something *once* is enough to become a memory that will stay with the child forever. There's a quotation in the front of my Bible copied from Rod McKuen: "I know only the dying heart needs the nourishment of memory to live beyond too many winters." On days of snow and wind and biting cold, days when my heart tends to despair, memories of my father's patience come to me. And I love him completely.

As a father it is not *what* are you waiting for?
but *who* are you waiting for?

TWENTY-THREE

LOST AND FOUND

✦✦✦✦✦✦✦✦✦

Holiness lies spread and borne over the surface
of time and stuff like color.

—*Annie Dillard*

SUNSHINE, WHAT'S UP?

Obviously she's up and it's after 9:30 P.M. and you'd hoped
she was asleep. But she's waiting for you with a grin on her
face and hope in her eyes.

Look, Dad.

She wide-mouth grins and leans to one side so I can clearly see the space where a tooth used to be. The hole is full of bright red blood; there are stains of the same hue on the towel she's holding.

Mom said to put it in the tooth fairy pillow. Bye!

I watch her bounce down the hall toward her bedroom. She may have her doubts about the tooth fairy, but for today she's a believer. My mind immediately registers that I don't have any cash, nothing, nada. This is not an uncommon experience for me. I commiserate with the missus and she's broke too.

And so you find yourself traipsing off to Safeway at 10 P.M. to get coffee and potatoes and some cash. And you're driving back home at 10:14 P.M. and the bank sign says 53 degrees and the town is drowsy and you're glad to be alive. Broke, but glad to be alive.

And you begin to get misty. You think about the little girl with a blood red hole in her mouth, how she struggles some days with being in the middle. You're thinking about the tooth she lost tonight and about the things she will lose in days to come: friends, maybe boyfriends (my lord), hopes, dreams, pieces of her identity, maybe even herself if something tragic occurs. You get choked up because tonight, at 10:14 P.M. and 53 degrees, the thing she just lost will grow back, good as new.

And for now, you, her dad, have the power to quietly, skill-fully, slide some cash under her pillow and make it even bet-ter. You're misty-eyed because you know as sure as coffee and potatoes that days will come when the tooth fairy will fly away for good and she will come to you with something she's lost and you'll stand there before this middle girl you love so much. And for all your strength and will, you will not be able to make it all better, help her find something that will grow back, good as new.

And so I close the garage, quietly put the groceries away, and count out two dollars. I gather up my wits, put on my wings, and fly to her room to do my best tooth fairy. She doesn't move a muscle. I've gotten good at this.

> Seize the days when you can be the hero
> for days will come when you'll have to be
> human.

TWENTY-FOUR

AGAIN AND AGAIN

✤✤✤✤✤✤✤✤✤

Showering, shampooing, brushing the teeth,
taking a multivitamin, going for a daily walk,
as unremarkable as they seem, are acts of
self-respect.

—*Kathleen Norris*

I TUCKED THREE CHILDREN into bed and they
untucked themselves three times after that, again. I fed the
Beta fish, *Stella*, with three little pellets of life, again. Not
long after, I spent twenty minutes in my target zone, again,

followed by a few push-ups. A quick shower followed after which I took my sweaty-target-zone clothes downstairs to the laundry basket, again.

I kissed my wife and she said *I love you*, again. I said *I love you back*.

The Beagle awoke at 11:47 P.M., crying to go outside, again. I got up and let him out and he relieved himself and quickly came back inside and went straightway to his pen and went to sleep, again.

I awoke at 3:45 A.M., interiorly crying to go to the bathroom, again. I got up and attended to business, again. I went back to bed, and just lay there for about fifteen minutes, again.

A little after 4:30 A.M., I read the daily psalms from *The Book of Common Prayer*, again. The coffeemaker clicked on at 4:45 A.M., again. When the coffeemaker finished, again I poured a cup in the pottery mug she bought me a few Christmases ago. A level spoonful of brown sugar and an intentional stir with a plastic spoon, again, so as to not wake her and the tucked-in kids and the relieved Beagle.

About 6:30 A.M., wool socks and boots, again. My son and I will leave at 7:10 A.M. and drive to his middle school, again. Just before leaving, I'll kiss my wife and say *I love you*, again. She'll say *I love you back*.

I'll drive my old beater to work and do what needs to be done, again.

And here's the absolute kick-in-the-head: I'll be anxious all day to get back home, to these repetitions, as unremarkable as they may seem, for they are acts of self-respect, enhancing my ability to take pleasure in myself, and in this world, yet once again.

There's a line from a Dixie Chicks song, "the freedom of my chains." I know of this freedom, and I know of these chains. It is impossible to have one without the other; trying is insanity, a form of suicide.

> The daily sets of repetitions are what keep
> you healthy and make you stronger for the
> long road ahead.

TWENTY-FIVE

TIME OUT #2

✦✦✦✦✦✦✦✦✦

JEFFREY BROWN: In the forward, when you're describing writing short stories, you write, "My only duty was to describe reality as it had come to me, to give the mundane its beautiful due." What does that mean, to give the mundane its beautiful due?

JOHN UPDIKE: You know, I worked hard at that sentence, 'cause I was trying, you know, having challenged myself to say, "What did I think I was doing?", I then had to find the phrases for it. But I've always had, I think, even before I began to publish, this notion that the ordinary middle-class life was enough to write about, that there was enough drama, interest, relevance, importance, poetry in it.[2]

To give the mundane its beautiful due. Updike penned that phrase as the writer's duty. I believe it is also the father's duty. In some sense, it may very well be the human duty. As indicated in the last chapter, life is full of repetition, again and again and again. True, it appears that some people live a life of 24/7 swashbuckling adventure with never a boring cloud in sight, but the emphasis there is on the word *appears*.

I believe behind the appearances lies the truth. Most days life is ordinary, if not quite mundane. But that ordinariness is, in Updike's words, "enough." There is enough there that calls for bravery and risk on the father's part as well as the mother and the child. And if you can learn to approach the ordinary as sufficient, then you'll never be sitting around whining "isn't there more to life?" It boils down to perspective, or how you see.

The insatiable quest for the next big thing is exactly that—insatiable, never satisfied. It may be a hoot to visit Disneyland, but I'm not sure anyone wants to live there. A part of being a father is discovering the magic kingdom in your own backyard or brownstone or corner condo or wherever. And again, it has to do with your eyes.

An old grandmotherly type once told me, "Never miss the opportunity to show your babies the moon." Yes, that's what she said: "the moon." For most of us the moon is superordinary, we seldom give it the time of day. Yet that simple practice brought beauty to my life and the life of my kids when they were very young. I'd love to tell you I never missed an opportunity to show them the moon, but I can't.

But I did try my best to take them to the window or walk out on the steps and point at the hole in the night sky and say, "Look."

Give the mundane its beautiful due. Try your best to point and say, "Will you look at that?"

TWENTY-SIX

QUIVER-FULL

✦✦✦✦✦✦✦✦✦

Like arrows in the hand of a warrior

are the children of one's youth.

Happy is the man
who has his quiver full of them.

He shall not be put to shame

when he speaks with his enemies in the gate.

—*Psalm 127:4-5*

THE WARRIOR WITH THE quiver-full (me) sat in the middle of my middle girl's room as she did homework, happy. It was one of those bundles of moments when, at least in my mind, time slows like molasses. You begin seeing things as if they're still life. Homework girl had just put on my old Vanessa Carlton CD because she knows I like it. And that's when I saw their feet.

First homework girl's. I guess when I wasn't looking she grew into young girl's feet, almost a woman's. They're daintily solid, they'll hold her weight. She was moving around the room with authority, this middle child, dancing to the music while cleaning her bookshelf, readying herself for Monday and beyond. *Girl, you're almost a woman now*, as Neil sorta sang. She talks to me like she's the only child of my youth in the room. This is nothing new.

Then my youngest daughter came to sit near the door of the room she shares with homework girl. She was reading a book, to herself, with legs crossed and bare feet pointing northish and southish; she was reading *Junie B. Jones*. She had been outside earlier while I was cleaning up Beagle poop in the yard. She was barefooted. *Git some shoes on, crazy! You see all this stuff I'm cleaning up? If you stepped in it and happened to have a cut on your foot, it could get infected and you'd incur huge medical bills.* Later, near the doorway, I didn't notice any cuts or poop or latent infection on her feet. No, just happy toes that moved to Vanessa's voice, metronomes for this warrior's heart.

Finally, out of the blue he walked in, my son. He came and snuggled up beside me. This is not rare, but it's not an everyday occurrence. His bare feet (we do own shoes; it's just late in the evening and we're from Arkansas, relaxed and summer-cool) were propped up against the wall. Big, man feet, he has. His mother clipped his toenails last night; now, he's not quite so feral. It is the classic struggle with his mother: feral vs. *my baby*. His hair has grown beyond motherly standards and he's reading a lot of *Wolverine* comics. I, the happy warrior, understand.

As the Good Book says, happy is the man. I found myself, as the psalmist would say, sitting in the gate with no shame, with the feet of the children of my youth all at my feet. Happy indeed is the man.

One day, sooner I'm sure than I want, the warrior will send beautiful-bare-footed arrows from his bow into the plans prepared for them. But for now we sit in the gate as Vanessa sings and we read and talk and our feet move in a fascinating rhythm and we are happy.

> The beautiful is usually
> right there at your feet.

TWENTY-SEVEN

MADONNA AND CHILD

✦✦✦✦✦✦✦✦✦

What I fear now is that I will somehow miss
the point of living
here at all, living here between the dreaming
and the coming true.

—*Robert Benson*

MOVEMENT IN THE REARVIEW mirror drew my attention. A madonna and child in a minivan. She was driving even while talking on her cell phone and waving her arms in the air like some conductor. That was the movement that caught my eyes. A little boy was sitting in the passenger seat, head turned away from her and her opus, looking out the window, silently, quietly.

Seconds earlier I had been listening to Yo-Yo Ma suck the marrow out of some song via his *Domenico Montagnana 1733* cello. Ma has nicknamed it *Petunia*. Aspen and oak along the street were dropping their skirts of gold and red; they stood naked and unashamed. A dog was walking his man down the sidewalk. The man breathed in and out and I could see his effort, such was the temperature. They were seconds of being painfully aware of beauty, of the world being shot straight through with the grandeur of God. And then a red light, and I stopped and saw them—harried madonna and child.

Do you ever have that feeling where you just know what's going on? Not details, but a pretty good sense of the general state of affairs?

Yo-Yo Ma lovingly drew his bow across *Petunia's* belly as the last note raged against the dying of the red light. Suddenly I was furious. I believe if there's anything at all that God will judge us for it will be our stiff-necked refusal to recognize the gifts he's given, some of them sitting in the passenger seat beside us looking out the window, silently, quietly. We pray and ask for the wrong things, when the right things are sitting quietly beside us. We'd be better off shutting up and shutting it down, whatever *it* is, and glancing over to the passenger seat at the handiwork of God looking longingly out the window.

We'd pay good money and give our eye teeth to actually be touched by an angel when they're in our own backyard swinging, created by God, created just a little lower than God, and they're flying higher and higher, all angel-like, and smiling and laughing. And us? We're distracted by the ten thousand things we just know are necessary for the world to keep a'turnin'.

Green light. *Petunia* begins to ache the theme from *Once Upon a Time in the West.* My breathing slowed. And I ached with *Petunia.* I ached for distracted madonna and the little girl she used to be and the moments when she possibly sat as a little girl in the passenger seat, silently, quietly. I ached for the little boy not two feet from her, all buckled up and safe, yet quite possibly full of a fear that only a mother's words could calm. I ached for me and for all the moments when there are angels in my backyard or in the car or sitting on my lap and I'm off conducting my own godforsaken private symphony. And I ached for us, for all of us, as we're barreling toward Babylon at the speed of distraction while aspens drop their skirts and men obediently follow dogs and little boys dream of small talk with their mothers.

Merci. Mercy.

> I fear God will judge us one of
> these days for our stiff-necked
> refusal to recognize the gifts he's given.

TWENTY-EIGHT

YESTERDAY'S TIME

✦✦✦✦✦✦✦✦✦

I view any encounter with a wild animal in
its own territory as a gift, an opportunity to
sense the real animal.

—*Barry Lopez*

1. LAST NIGHT MY SON performed in his first band
concert. Sixth grade. Trumpet. He and his compadres did a
great job. Well, to be truthful, the percussion section had a
tendency to rush things, but such are the ways of drummers
with youth in their veins. I watched as awkward hands and

fingers on the end of awkward arms concentrated as if our country's welfare depended on them. Right feet kept time with the conductor's baton. The sixth-graders played *Fly's in the Buttermilk* and *Frere Jacques*. The seventh-graders played *Another One Bites the Dust*. And the eighth-graders played Barber's *Adagio*. If that's not the spectrum I don't know what is.

2. I bent down yesterday morning to give my youngest daughter a goodbye kiss. She was still somewhat asleep, but I had to go. I kissed her forehead and sleepy eyes opened. As she reached up to kiss my nose her aim was low and she accidentally kissed my lips. Her eyes grew wide as saucers and a big smile broke her face. *Bye, Dada.*

3. I listened last night as my middle daughter announced over spaghetti and french bread *No homework for me!* She declared this as her mother's earrings dangled from her ears, silver hoops. I'm not too fond of those silver hoops as they make my middle daughter look a little too grown up, kinda like that preacher's daughter from *Footloose*. I know she wants to be seen, noticed. Who doesn't? Little does she know that you almost cannot help seeing her, such is her beauty; she is like elf-light. Last night, at the band concert, she leaned in and put her head, earrings and all, on my shoulder.

As I try hard to keep pace with the passage of time I wonder if my children know the extent, the blessed depth, of my affection for them?

Skip to my Lou, my darlings . . .

Children deserve to be seen
in their natural habitats.
This allows us to sense
who they really are.

TURNING BACK

Raised in the half-light of grace with a father
and mother and brother and dog and nightly
meals together and 'I love you, good night'
every night, without fail. A world awash with
the wonder of Kraft spaghetti dinners and
Rod McKuen on the phonograph and the way
rain smells falling through pine trees and
for God so loved the world and Brian's Song.
Judged by today's standards it looks naive,
almost fanciful, a nostalgia best left to reruns.
But turning back I find it deeply cunning, a time
guided by love, an extended session in deliberation,
a careful refusal to hurry though the shadows
were drawing then as they do now. Was it a
white-bread-King-James-horn-rimmed life?
Those are the hyphenated categories of a fool.
You see it was my life, the dream I still dream and
find increasing gratitude for every day, without fail.

TWENTY-NINE

NEW YEAR'S EVE

✦✦✦✦✦✦✦✦✦

Just for a moment I was back at school

—*Dan Fogelberg*

WHEN I WAS HOME recently my mom asked me to go through some boxes, boxes of my life. She wondered if any of it might be thrown away; I said *no, I'd like to hang on to it all*. Sitting on the shelf near the boxes of memories was a metal rack full of 45 rpm records. I used to buy those things for ninety-nine cents, much like my kids buy songs on iTunes today.

I took the rack of miniature nostalgia over to the record player and started spinning the soundtrack of my youth. The Moody Blue's *Gemini Dream*; Steve Winwood's *While You See a Chance*; Survivor's *Eye of the Tiger*; Mellencamp's *Jack and Diane*; and of course, Fogelberg's *Old Lang Syne*. There was just something right about seeing the slow descent of the needle and then that *snap*, *crackle*, *pop* as the vinyl slowly bled the magic. Yeah, I'm not sure my analog heart is going to fully make the digital conversion.

Auld Lang Syne. Loosely translated—*good old days*. That's where the music took me. Just for a moment I was back at school, back to grade school and junior high and high school and monogrammed sweaters and Levi 501s and reading *A Separate Peace* and bus trips to football games and scrubbing your face so the acne didn't go ape on you and carrying a long-handled comb in your back pocket and braces and *Members Only* jackets and lifting weights so you wouldn't stay so skinny and sitting behind Misty Bedford in algebra class while thinking about everything *but* solving for *x* and going to the army surplus store to buy fatigues for three dollars and sitting on the steps of Pine Street Junior High after lunch just trying to be cool and drinking raw eggs like Rocky did and Ocean Pacific T-shirts and dancing like a white guy (step forward, step back, step forward, step back) and pep rallies and driving a '67 Chevy pickup with a column shift and a boom box strapped to the top of the seat and picking out 45 rpms at the record store . . .

Some of those boxes my mom asked me to look through did have things in them that could've been thrown away.

But I want to keep it all—as though it all mattered and all fit together to make my life. Some of those musically induced good old days were actually days of pain: all Misty Bedford wanted me for was algebra answers; the weights and raw eggs never really transformed me into Rocky; the braces were metal railroads on my teeth my senior year of high school.

The temptation on New Year's Eve is to get all gussied up on Korbel and convert our analog lives to digital, to something cleaner, less scratchy. That temptation seems to grow greater with each passing year.

Today I want to resist that temptation and I pray the same for my kids when their time comes to clean out (or not) their set of boxes. As hard as it may be, I pray we all have some time, if just for a moment, to let the needle pull the *snap*, *crackle*, *pop* out of the vinyl of our lives and remember where we've been.

I'm not sure any of us know where we're going, what the future holds; nobody's been there yet. But most of us know where we've been, the lives we've lived and who we've become in the living of those days. And if I or you or we should remember that old familiar pain, then so be it. It reminds us that once, we were here.

When those times come to clean,

let your children decide what to throw away

and what to keep.

THIRTY

A REAL BOY

✦✦✦✦✦✦✦✦✦

There was once upon a time . . .
"A king!" my little readers
will instantly exclaim.
No, children, you are wrong. There was once
upon a time a piece of wood.

—*C. Collodi*

I ASKED HIM IF HE thought his mother and I would approve. Through downcast eyes filled with middle school hair he said, *No, Dad . . . I just thought you wouldn't find out.*

Our arrangement had been I take him to school in the mornings and he rides the bus home in the afternoon. Simple, clean, safe. But then one day his mother saw him walking home with some boys. The story, which we believe, was he missed the bus and saw the neighborhood boys walking and caught up with them. Another story unfolded. That it happened once before, not due to missing a bus, but at the invite of these boys. Some of you might think *good lord, Pop, what's the problem?* But he's not yours, he's mine.

In my mind's eye, my boy was essentially walking alongside Fox and Cat, those two characters who led Pinocchio astray, telling him to plant his money in the Field of Miracles or something. The truth is my boy was walking alongside a couple of boys.

As we sat in his bedroom, I, also a firstborn who didn't tell my parents everything, said *I'd give my life for you, bud, no questions asked. Walking home like that puts you at risk. For a little while longer, I've got the responsibility to at least try and make sure you're safe.* And then his tears fell. Mine did too. Two firstborns who didn't and still won't tell our parents everything, sitting there in our tears lost in the awkward dance steps of fathers and sons and sons and fathers.

My firstborn son is on the long road home. So am I. So are we all.

Later that night, just before surrendering to sleep, I remembered a time when I was a boy, getting into a pickup with Lightbulb. Oh, that wasn't his name, but that's what we called him. I guess we just as easily could've called him Fox or Cat. I was probably my son's age, if not younger. Lightbulb took me for a pickup ride on a stretch of highway between two sleepy little towns where boredom grew long like middle school hair. The speedometer reached 80, 85, 90 . . . *just a little more, Lightbulb* . . . 100 mph. We flew like bats in a black stepside Chevrolet. He held that speed the length of a Field of Miracles, and I felt a real boy.

Be responsible and leave the porch light on.
There's no way you can know everything.

THIRTY-ONE

A GOOD MAN

✦✦✦✦✦✦✦✦✦

> This story shall the good man
> teach his son; . . .
>
> From this day to the ending of the world,
>
> But we in it shall be remember'd;
>
> We few, we happy few, we band of brothers.
>
> —*Shakespeare, Henry V, Act IV, scene III*

MY SON TURNED TWELVE years old on Tuesday. And so begins his first steps into becoming a man. We celebrated his life with traditional cards, gifts, and his meal of choice: pot roast and potatoes. But I wanted to do something with him on the weekend, just the two of us, to mark time; to officially begin the days.

A good man offered the use of his cabin nearby. This is fitting as the friend uses this cabin for rite-of-passage ceremonies for boys, initiating them into manhood. Will and I drove there, stopping at a local place to order a twenty-pack of wings and "killer seasoned fries." Then we snaked up hills until coming to our destination.

After the meal, which left us farting all night, we went upstairs and sat down for the main event: HBO's miniseries *Band of Brothers*, all of it.

Several months ago I'd felt that we, my son and I, would need a common language or story to use as a foundation for his days ahead. I grew up watching westerns with my dad, it is our common story: *Monte Walsh, The Cowboys, Lonesome Dove*. At my father-in-law's house over Christmas, Will saw one episode of *Band of Brothers* on the History Channel; he sat transfixed. In that moment, I knew what our story needed to be, or at least could be.

A part of me is sad that my son has not warmed to westerns. I remind myself that the intent is not to help him become a cowboy or a soldier, but a man. The hero's journey is the same, whether it's Stetsons or helmets. So off to Normandy we went.

I firmly believe that the soul of a boy, much like the soul of a man, is shy if not downright skittish. You can slowly draw it out into the open and any jerky move can send it skittering back into the shadows. I wanted the evening to be as natural as possible, for fear that overt actions to help a boy "get it" send him running.

What I'm interested in is my son's soul, that deepest part of his life. My son and I do a lot together, so it's not like an absent father coming in for a weekend and trying to give him the goods before shipping off again. No, ours is *as we go*. But this was intentional, a step toward manhood.

We watched a little, talked a little, laughed a little, and cringed a little. I watched to see what character he would be drawn to; just my luck, "Wild Bill" Guarnere, the roughneck from Philly with a mouth to make even Southern Baptist mothers pray the rosary. Oh, he liked some of the others as well, but "Wild Bill" made his soul peek out, I saw it. After a few episodes, I asked why he liked this character. *He's a good man, Dad.* And I warmed on the inside, and thanked the Grace that keeps this world for a moment when you hear the answer you long to hear.

And so we have our benchmark: a good man. That's what, in my better moments, I hope I am, and that's what I pray my son will become. That's what my dad is. And it's what Wild Bill was. I have heard, especially in the christian community, that it's not enough to just be a good man; that you've gotta be *God's man* or something like that. Maybe that's why I believe most of the loud male christian voices know precious little about the soul of a man, let alone their own. If you bristle at that statement, well, so be it.

There was a time when the world asked ordinary men to do extraordinary things. I believe we are still in that time. The world needs good men. That's why we carry on, my son and I, a little at a time, toward the mark.

The world needs good men.

SOMETHING

It's important to be good at something.
The something is not as important
as the fact that you're good at it.
You could be a circus master
or a gynecologist,
either one's fine
as long as you're good.
Of course you could choose
to be a man, a good man.
Now that's something important.

THIRTY-TWO

FIVE THINGS

✦✦✦✦✦✦✦✦✦

Teach your children well . . .

—*Graham Nash*

HERE ARE FIVE THINGS my father taught me, either directly or indirectly. Why five? Because five represents a handful, any more than that and it gets hard to handle.

1. It's good to love. Folks remember little of what you say or do, but they do remember what you love. The texture of your life comes from your loves. My dad loves my mom, and Johnny Cash music, and horses, and peanut butter. If you love people

and places and even things, your heart'll break many times over. Sure, there are bad breaks, but there are also good breaks. You'll never know the difference unless you choose to love.

2. It's good to have some heroes besides Jesus. Keep Jesus by all means, but a little faith in fellow feet of clay demonstrates you live in the world and not just on it. One of my dad's heroes died recently—James Arness, aka Marshall Dillon. His death broke my dad's heart, just a little. My dad's heroes have always been cowboys, and Jesus.

3. It's good to be moved to tears. When heroes die or when the national anthem is played at ball games or when you lay eyes on your grandkids for the very first time. Not too long ago I sat with my dad and brother and we listened to the soundtrack from *True Grit*, those old hymns rendered achingly gorgeous by Carter Burwell. My dad just sat there and wept. Then I did too.

4. It's good to go easy on folks. That tough love stance is appropriate every once in a while, sorta like that singular incident of Jesus kicking over stuff in the Temple. But that's the exception. The rule worth more than gold is this: be gentle.

5. It's good to remember God speaks through the sacred. And if all of life is sacred, then God speaks through everything. The trick is to learn to listen to the whole show, every single stitch of it, all of this world's heartbreaking beauty. Then, when the end comes, and it will, you can smile and say *my, my* and mean it.

> Of all the things you've got to remember
> I suggest at least these five.
> Why? Because life's a handful.

A LITTLE SPACE

In his early thirties Blake wrote
that line about learning to bear
the beams of love. It is the kind of
phrase you turn in the pride of life.
Lately I've wondered what William
would have penned had he waited
until the space of his forties, when he
was a little more bereav'd of light.
My mid-forty gut tells me his thought
might have been more along lines of
learning to bear the burden of nouns,
like bodies and cloud and lambs and God.

THIRTY-THREE

TIME OUT #3

✦✦✦✦✦✦✦✦✦

The held breath. As if we haven't quite
begun yet to exist . . .
That final form just waiting,
the world waiting.

—*B. H. Fairchild*

4 A.M., I STEPPED OUT on the back stoop to wake myself up, to splash my bare chest with cold. Everything in sight was agog with moonglow. I looked up and into the night's full sun, and out of that splendid orb came a voice I

believe to be God's and God said *tell the parents to breathe.* And so I am.

Breathe. Don't hold your breath any longer. Begin to exist today fully. Begin today to inhale and exhale the fullness of you. We half-exist most days based on contingencies—*I'll begin when the kids are grown and gone* or *when we're in better financial shape* or *when there is consensus on the team.* We are a blue-faced race holding our breath most days, waiting and waiting. And why? At the risk of offending or inspiring you, I wager an answer: because we are afraid.

Holding back—it is the mortal sin of omission. A fearful half-existence of omitting our very selves from a world dappled with divine grace. A pinching held-breath stumbling through day after day grasping at the black hope of *one of these days* . . . and all too often that day never comes, or when it finally does it's over and we stand before the night's full sun and a voice comes from inside that splendid orb and asks *why were you afraid?*

In that moment our bare bodies will be splashed with the cold-ache of a stillborn life. Oh there will be mercy, no doubt . . . but mercy bittered with regret.

Breathe.

THIRTY-FOUR

I LOVE YOU

＋＋＋＋＋＋＋＋＋

so this bell calls us all . . .

—*John Donne*

IT WAS SUNDAY MORNING coming down in Phoenix. I was there on business. My wife called early that morning saying *they don't think Dad's going to make it; I need to go.* A little while later the cell phone rang and her voice held two words: *He's dead.*

Her dad's name was John. He'd been fighting pancreatic cancer. Then pneumonia crept in and he was just too weak. The writer Barry Lopez describes your death day as the day "the river calls your name." That Sunday the river called John's name.

My wife told me *I got to talk to him . . . they put the phone to his ear and I said I love you, Dad.* For that I am thankful. When someone dies alone, all they hear is the river; and while it's possible you might hear angels or harps, I would think it could also be frightening, cold, lonely. But in addition to whatever sound was in my father-in-law's ears was a daughter's voice: *I love you, Dad.*

As I flew back to Denver, she flew out to Arkansas. She called again. My voice carried four closing words: *I love you, Meredith.*

Psychological literati skewer that "I love you" phrase, saying *if you don't really feel it, you shouldn't say it.* That's about the stupidest thing I've ever heard. You don't say it because you're trying to get the inside to match the outside; you say those words because the river always flows and you never know when it might call your name or the name of someone you love. Saying "I love you" is insurance; to not carry it is the stuff of which regrets are made.

One of the most precious human gifts we give one another is to do what we can to ensure others know the grace of our intentions, that we intend to be loving and kind even when we may not act like it or feel it. That's the reason I strive to tell my wife and my kids *I love you* every day, without fail. Because you never know what any given Sunday may bring.

Tell 'em *I love you*, everyday.
Just say the words, because you never know.

THIRTY-FIVE

SOFTLY AND TENDERLY

+++++++++

Softly and tenderly Jesus is calling,
calling for you and for me . . .

THE CHILDREN WHO CALL ME dad have been with their grandparents, two people who call me son. On this particular Sunday, Papa the preacher gave the normally expected invitation at the conclusion of his sermon. In the Baptist tradition, this is a time to be quiet and respond to the Spirit of God, maybe even deciding to walk down an aisle, take the preacher's hand, and "be saved."

See, on the portals he's waiting and watching,
watching for you and for me . . .

My father stood before the people and pleaded for some-one to come to Jesus. But no one did, no one until my middle girl looked at her grandmother and asked, "Can I go?"

Come home, come home, you who are weary, come home . . .

As the story goes, my middle girl reached my father's pastoral hands and she broke down, tears and all. A bit later, after the saving moment, after the church service, after lunch, my mother called me to tell me what had happened.

Earnestly, tenderly, Jesus is calling, calling,
O sinner, come home!

Then, soon after, my middle girl called me. "Daddy, I believe in God and Jesus, you know that. But Daddy, Papa was so sad that no one was coming, he looked so sad. I just had to go, Daddy. I just had to go for Papa."

On that Sunday morning I believe a preacher stood, as is his custom, and prayed that an angel would come and stir the waters in an old and familiar routine. And so an angel did; she stepped out into the eyes and whispers of saints and sinners alike and shed almost every shred of her own pride and humbled herself for Papa's sake, for love's sake . . . for Christ's sake. And when she finally reached his hands, she emptied herself for him, tears and all. In its original Latin form *sacrifice* means *to make sacred* or *to make holy*. That's what my daughter did both for my father and for the time that day.

On my swing from branch to branch up the tree of God, there is an oft-heard bark: *only Jesus saves!* I understand that. I also believe we save each other from time to time, maybe even many more times than we're aware. But the angels always see. On a Sunday not long ago, I believe the angels paused their endless praise and looked on in envy as the race of sinners and middle girls got just a few steps closer to home.

To sacrifice is to make sacred.

It is how the days are made holy.

THIRTY-SIX

COMMUNION

✦✦✦✦✦✦✦✦✦

It was music which first awakened me to the
need for reflection.

—*Henry Bugbee*

MY FATHER WOULD RISE EARLY of a morning before
sun and sons and wife. His ritual was to stack the albums he
loved and then let the needle slowly drop. The volume would
be barely a whisper at the beginning; every five minutes or
so he would stroll back by and increase the sound slightly,
smoothly. While other houses were roused by alarm clocks of

bells or beeps, our home gradually simmered each morning in the juice of music: Johnny Cash, Sons of the Pioneers, the gentleman Jim Reeves, Rod McKuen, Ray Conniff.

As that cheap needle drew crackled sound from warm vinyl, so were my brother and I drawn from sleep to face the day.

Those morning ministrations were priestly; you cannot convince me otherwise.

As I grew older I spent prodigal days with Cougar Mellencamp and Boston and Journey. I stepped away from my father's music. But now, in my forties, probably the age he was in the days of my youth, I have found an AM station that plays Glen Campbell and Tom T. Hall and Andy Williams . . . and Cash, always Cash.

Each morning now I listen on my commute and think of my father and his genius. How in the world did he come up with such a brilliant way of waking his sons? Did he even realize what he was doing? Had he the foggiest notion that his music was our morning communion, a discipline that made sure we started the day warm and filled?

Back then I thought my father's music was just that— music. But now I know differently. He was entrusted with the care of our souls, and he made sure we knew it's good to touch the green, green grass of home.

Yes, that first meal of the day
may be the most important. Start well.

RESOLVE

What do you do when you discover
your inheritance is too small for you,
that all your instruction and training
were intended to create the guts for
you to say I'm leaving now, goodbye?
The far country doesn't have to be a
place of wasting; it can be a horizon
of spending yourself in extravagant
gestures never dreamed of by your
father and his father before him. You
must not look your father in his eyes
as you walk away. He knows you are
his son but you are also the offspring of
wild, rangy, boom-bust ancestors who
would not suffer fences. He knows there
will be no tableau of homecoming,
yet his shoulders rise with sorrow's pride.

THIRTY-SEVEN

GREAT RESPONSIBILITY

❖❖❖❖❖❖❖❖❖

That is at bottom the only courage that is
demanded of us . . .

—*Ranier Maria Rilke*

MY SON TURNS THIRTEEN tomorrow.

One evening, a little over a week ago now, I walked into his bedroom and saw him at the computer. As I did, my Spidey-sense went off; where you know danger is near. We have clear rules regarding "online."

Have you been looking at something you shouldn't have been? This is one of those moments when it's really important to tell the truth.

His face told me the answer, then his mouth followed. I shut his bedroom door and sat the edge of his bed.

Why don't you show me what you've been looking at.

He protested, trying to explain that he'd been searching Google images. The boys at school had been feeding him tales of sexy girls online.

He protested a little more—as I said, he turns thirteen tomorrow. But I gently protested even more; I turn forty-three in about a month.

Why don't you take me where you've been. We'll go together.

And so my son showed me the pages he'd been viewing, a screen full of images along the lines of the *Sports Illustrated* swimsuit issue, nothing he hasn't seen watching *Dancing with the Stars* or in *Avatar*'s 3D. I looked at the search box to see what he had typed: "sexy girl hollywood movie star models." The innocence in that moment was almost too much for me; my son was struggling even for the lingo to type.

We gotta be real careful here, man. This can take you to some dark places, fast, too fast.

The heart of our conversation after that is just between father and son. It is an ongoing one. The two of us are going out this evening; it will continue then. I don't want to diminish in any way the gravity of those moments. The stories of porn addiction seem to be legion these days, more often than not starting at about his age. Our cultural landscape is littered with abuse, wrecked marriages, pain.

My almost-thirteen-year-old son is wrestling with his self, his mind, his body, his very soul, and how those facets of who he is fit together. It's never smooth.

These wrestlings do not go away. I know. I'm almost forty-three. Yes, yes, that apostle said we wrestle not with flesh and blood, but some days I'd swear he was lying.

In the wake of that evening, I felt another conversation going on, between the Good Father and me.

God: We gotta be real careful here, John. This is about his heart. And yours.

Me: I know. Please help me. Please. I'm not Spiderman.

God: Trust your gut, your senses. It's a great responsibility.

Me: It is great getting to be his dad, isn't it?

God: You can do this.

> Fathering our children is a
> great responsibility.
> It doesn't come any greater.

THE RAVEN AND DOVE

I drive them to school each morning of my own free
will. Sometimes we're quiet, still slowly waking up.
Other times we're noisy, laughing at the schools of
prairie dogs along our lanes all with rapt attention
as we sail by. Our speed dwindles to 20 mph on the
final approach, then that pregnant pause as the great
hull opens and the raven and dove fly away.
There are times they turn to catch my eye, glances
I cherish. There are other times they don't look back.
But with each release I further sympathize with the
old captain, with Noah's tangled desire from the bow:
fly straight. find the hope. please don't forget me.

THIRTY-EIGHT

WHAT I WANT YOU TO KNOW

✦✦✦✦✦✦✦✦✦

My dear children,

You know I read a lot of Jim Harrison and he uses this line, *only God knows how much I love you,* in several of his novels. Harrison stole that line from Gabriel Garcia Marquez, who no doubt stole it from somebody else. Anyway, only God knows how much I love you. I'm proud of the three of you, I truly am. You're sweet to kids younger than you and respectful to those old enough to be your grandparents. I believe we as a people are known by how we treat the very young and the very old and, based on that, you guys are battin' a thousand.

I realize some evenings I fall asleep watching television with you. I'm sorry. I used to wonder why my grandfather did that of an evening, even my dad does that. Well, now I know why: they were worn slap out from working all day trying to give me something they didn't have and I'm not just talking about stuff. Those men, from whose cloth I'm cut, worked a full day to provide food, clothes, shelter, opportunities, and love. I believe they did it willingly, as do I, but I admit it wears on you. Some of that is no doubt due to that fruit-eating party in Eden; it's a heavy curse. Some days I'm strong, others I'm weak. On the weak days, just wipe the drool off my chin and please cover me up with a blanket.

I so want you to know, deep within your marrow, that it's a wonderful life, that this crazy existence is pure gift and nothing else. Yes, there's a lotta suffering and sin and death and dying, but there are just as many lilacs blooming outside your windowsill and babies coming crying into this world so fresh from God and Gordon Lightfoot singing about the Edmund Fitzgerald. Sometimes you've gotta look for it, scratch hard; but the wonder is there, always, always, always.

I pray one of these days, when I'm dead and gone, that you'll sit around and say *Daddy sure loved this world, didn't he?* And one of you will whisper *God only knows how much.*

Two quick things. I've noticed you fighting with each other in the house lately. It drives your mom plum batty, but I'm inclined to give you a little rein because I've seen you stand up for each other out there, in the neighborhood. I hope you'll always stand up for each other. You're *family* and that word means everything.

I want you to hang on to each other, come hell or high water. If and when you're married with kids, or even if you're not, I want you to call each other. I don't do that enough with my brother and it grieves my heart because only God knows how much I love him. I'm trying to call him more often. And while you're at it, call your parents too; you don't have to talk long, just let us hear your glorious voices so we know you're all right. That's really what we want, what we've always wanted, to know you're all right.

AND remember, as Spiderman teacheth us, that *with great power comes great responsibility.* I like to amend that slightly with the addition of the word *love* . . . so, **with great love comes great responsibility**. You've been born into a loving family. Be gentle with people. I believe most folks just want to be loved, maybe God only knows how much.

<blockquote>With great love comes great responsibility.</blockquote>

LETTERS FOR DAD-O

Her third grade spelling list for the week includes
the words *dance*, *wreck*, *fancy*, and *tremble*.
She already knows how to spell them,
she'll ace Friday's test, "no prob, dad-o."
Still, we'll review them, just to be sure.
As she reels off *d-a-n-c-e*
I see a boy who will one day soon
take heart and ask her to inhabit this word.
Maybe he'll grow on me, I doubt it.
W-r-e-c-k will be the letters soaked in tears
as she explains "I swerved to miss the dog, dad-o,
but I'm o.k."
Thank God and Jesus.
I'm no prophet but my gut tells me
she'll want the *f-a-n-c-y* wedding dress,
her easy days of hoodies and jeans faded
like weekly spelling lists.
Still, just to be sure, we review these omens.
I try my best not to let her see me *t-r-e-m-b-l-e*.

THIRTY-NINE

THE OLD ONES

✦✦✦✦✦✦✦✦✦

They learned the recitations of seasons . . .

—*James Galvin*

THE RESTAURANT'S HOSTESS said about ten minutes, so we sat down and began to people-watch. I had just asked my wife *what do you think we'll look like when we're old?* when the couple approached us, an old couple, easily in their seventies. The lady asked if the seats next to us were taken, we said *no, please join us*. She sat down next to my wife and said *you sure are pretty*. She had dark hair like my wife. She held her hands in her lap. Her husband sat down and stared straight ahead, he and I bookends to the moment. He never said a word, but I felt he was listening.

She was a talker, an old whirlwind that still had a lotta whirl: *We have a ranch for sale in Salida, would you like to buy a ranch? . . . where are ya'll from? . . . we live in Santa Fe now, we come here to eat once a week . . . this is my husband John, he was in "the death march" (wink) . . . where are ya'll from? . . . the ranch in Salida has a red roof, you can see it as you top the hill . . . we both grew up in Texas . . . John always orders the combination plate . . . where are ya'll from? . . .*

We sat as she went through that loop twice and then again, the same statements, always the gentle refrain of *now where are ya'll from?* The mind, like the body, grows old. But for some the mind rages against the dying of the light, struggles to stay a part of life's conversation. I leaned in to ask deeper: *Your ranch sounds lovely, why are you selling it?* She looked at me as if I'd slapped her, knocked her off course. Tears welled in her eyes: *All the old ones are gone.* She peered at her lap and rubbed her hands, then looked back at me. I nodded gingerly, undone by her munificence. The hostess called our name, so we stood and said goodbye.

We ended up sitting just across from John and his wife. I stared from time to time, as writers tend to do. He ordered the combination plate, just like she said he would. The waiter seemed to recognize them, like maybe they dine there once every week, just like she said they did. John and his wife sat their entire meal in silence. There was a singular moment when he spoke, but not with words. When they initially arrived at their table, John pulled out her chair and allowed his wife to sit down, then pushed her up to her place. It was a tender gesture that spoke volumes to me, something an old one would do, an aged survivor who has a red-roofed ranch for sale in Salida with a wife who'd think nothing of telling a stranger *you sure are pretty.*

What do you think we'll look like when we're old? Little did I know the unraveling of my question that evening, little do any of us. It's funny, as I've had dreams before of owning a ranch near Salida . . . and my wife is a talker . . . and my name is John.

FORTY

DON'T FORGET US

✛✛✛✛✛✛✛✛✛

(a Baccalaureate speech)

D<small>EAR</small> G<small>RADUATES</small>,

I've been reading some of the speeches that came your way these last few weeks. My feeling is you've been subjected to the extremes. You've either heard *follow your heart/hitch your wagon to a star*, passionately presented by the peter pans of our culture who refuse to grow up . . . or *get married/ get a job/settle down*, boringly penned by the grown-ups constantly trying to gandydance America back on track. Mercy. I'm sorry about that, you're good sports to endure those trips to the poles. I'd like to offer you something from the middle, the speech I believe we really want you to hear as you step off into this thing called life, the prayer we whisper as you drive away: *please don't forget us*.

You see, we're scared you won't need us anymore. Oh, we're beaming with pride that you're swinging big and finding your drummer, and to think you're even considering sacred commitments, well, let's just say Jesus and David Brooks would be so proud. But please come home once in a while, bring the kids or your Rottweiler or your partner, stay a few days in the summer, holidays are nice too. Just don't forget us. Whether we did right by you or wrong by you, most days we tried our God-honest-best, or at least the best we knew how. We promise to try and treat you like adults but the truth is we still see you as children, the incarnation of the magnificent maybe . . . that maybe things can change, that maybe life will be a little different your time around. But if you never visit or e-mail, we'll be hounded by the recurring nightmare that hope is a fool's word, and we completely and utterly failed.

Now we don't want you to worry about us. We do have our own lives. A trip to Machu Picchu after the knee replacement. An eye on that little snowcone stand that's apparently in foreclosure. Possibly even turning your bedroom into an office. We've got dreams, no doubt about it. But you, you were always the best part of our beautiful American dream. So please don't worry about us, just please don't forget about us. You may recall we grew up listening to Glen Campbell's song "Gentle on My Mind"…that's all we want to be—gentle on your mind.

There you have it. Congratulations! Now go on. Change the world and be changed by it. Spend a decade or two trying to discover yourself while you spend Saturdays coaching T-ball and nights writing your screenplay. Introduce a friend to Vidalia onions and sleep with the window cracked when it rains. But don't overly fret about finding your specific life calling. Your calling is to a life, to live. And we believe this includes dropping in or calling home from time to time. You don't have to stay or talk long. Seeing your eyes or hearing your voice is like the dream reborn.

FORTY-ONE

YOUR LIFE

+++++++++

I ain't gonna spit on my whole life.

—*Monte Walsh*

I SAT IN THE SECOND row this morning as my son was confirmed in the Lutheran tradition. I had mixed feelings about the whole thing. I didn't know how it fit in our lives and as such how it might fit in his. You see, we're spiritual mutts. A mix of Southern Baptist, Catholic, non-denominational, and Anglican. Then, in an attempt to be *local* in all things, especially when our kids began middle school years, we joined a

Lutheran church in our town, in which our son and middle daughter began the confirmation journey.

I didn't want to overstate this day (not being born Lutheran), but at the same time I didn't want to underplay the importance of the faith steps my beloved son is taking in his one wild and precious life.

What's more true is that I've also been wrestling with angels all my own. I am a rover in the faith, a gypsy heart chasing the God of dusk, but I've so wanted to be constant, steadfast like my beautiful father. There's no shame there, it's just that my story hasn't played out as I thought it would.

This is true though. Jesus spoke to me this morning while I was eating Grape-Nuts Flakes and drinking coffee. He hijacked the first part of a verse I memorized as a boy—"Do not be ashamed of the gospel." That's all I heard. And like grace, that was sufficient. That breakfast epiphany prompted thoughts like what about *my* gospel, the gospel of *John*, the story of *my* life and my vagabondish days as ordered by an infinitely tender hand?

Jesus answered "Don't be ashamed of your life, John." He who hath ears let him hear.

So I sat in the second row this morning, a man with his nose rubbed in the amazement of grace. And I trembled when my grown-tall-boy knelt at the altar surrounded by parents and priests and his life was further sewn one-thread deeper into the fabric of God, that vast blanket in which I too am hemmed, as is my father. I had planned to pray many things over him in that spot of time, but there was only this: "Please God, may he not be ashamed of his life."

And so we mutt on, confirmed but not crushed, roving but not unto despair, debtors to grace, unashamed.

Whatever it looks like, it's yours.
Don't spit on your life.

FORTY-TWO

UPON MY OLDEST
DAUGHTER'S CONFIRMATION

✦✦✦✦✦✦✦✦✦

Confirmation = the process of supporting a
statement by evidence.

—*Merriam-Webster Dictionary*

MAYBE HALF THE GAME is being aware—of this day
and my daughter's words and the minister's red stole and the
chatter of family and relatives and the cross draped in white
linen high and lifted up above us all and those three candles
on the communion table that could have represented Father,

Son, and Holy Spirit or possibly Faith, Hope, and Love; but I have to tell you that for me for today those three candles stood for a father's plea: *Time, stand still.*

But time refused and maybe that's half the game too, being aware of the passing of time and enjoying it as it passes because it does you know. And passing the time well may be just about the most holy thing we do in this vale. For on that day someday when we hope to hear at least some variation of *Well done* my hunch is that it won't be for our accomplishments or trophies or accolades in any way but it may very well be for the way we sat still on days like today and listened to our daughters both recite a creed and renounce an evil they have little context for as of yet but they will grow into as we have. Yes, we belong to this world with all its flickering grandeur and yes, we belong to this time with all its fleeting beauty and yes, we belong to this day as do our daughters because there is a grace that keeps this world and holds us close as seasons pass. Amen.

Time doesn't stand still but grace keeps this
world and holds us close.

FORTY-THREE

DAYS THAT BUILD ME

✦✦✦✦✦✦✦✦✦

. . . and riot in things attainable.

—*John Keats*

I WENT WITH THE THREE females in my life. Their mother had warned me: you know they want bikinis, right? I had heard that word several times of late but had always tried to change the subject. For example,

Daughter: Dad, I really really want a bikini.
Me: Sweet-girl, have you finished reading Rob Bell's book yet?

Anyway, I went along yesterday, I felt it needed to be a father's day on some level. So I stood in a store known as Justice and leaned against a waiting-wall while three video screens assaulted my senses. I eyed my girls' feet below the 3/4 dressing room door, feet I know well, toes I've counted, this little piggy went to market. Their not-so-little-anymore feet skittered around accompanied by growing-girl giggles.

I don't know all about a hell, but I do believe in God because somehow my daughters' eyes were earlier drawn to that known as the tankini. Now I've nothing against bikinis, I'm rather fond of them in fact. But when you're a dad that fondness is tempered by that fact that you're a male and you know how fond males of any age are of girls sitting on chaise loungers in their bra and panties. I needed something for these middle-dad days I'm in, and that meant something to cover their-middle. *Voila!* Enter the tankini.

I stood up straight as I saw the dressing room door open. Two visions stepped forward to get my approval: *whaddaya think, Dad?* If they only knew what I thought. If they only knew my thrill at seeing their ear-wide grins, a thrill coupled with an extreme difficulty to breathe, sorta like my saddle shifting right underneath me. If they only knew how excited I am for the summer days they have ahead of them, while I so long for those seasoned days when I carried them both in my arms. *What do I think? Well, I like 'em. Let's get 'em.* And so we did. What a riot.

Yesterday was a day that built me, my daughters' father, just a little more. I may make it after all. The gentle irony was that our experience took place in that store called Justice. Any man worth his salt knows fathers are built by one thing and one thing only—*mercy.*

It's all about mercy.

FORTY-FOUR

A FATHER'S PRAYER

✦✦✦✦✦✦✦✦✦

OUR FATHER WHO IS ALWAYS NEAR,

I've seen them, heard them, felt them. They're chasing my children—the black riders. I believe with all I am that this world is shot straight through with breathtaking beauty. But I also know evil rides, often hardest after those so fresh from you, those I hold most dear. When they and I were young, I held them close and tight, in brightest day no evil did escape my sight. But we are all older now and they're roving beyond me, farther from the shire, as it is supposed to be.

And so I raise a prayer on this Father's Day eve, no doubt one your ears know well, one voiced by my father and my father's father . . . one I believe you too whispered for your only begotten as he laid his glory down and ventured into blackest night:

what grace is given me, let it pass to them.

Good Father, when the memory of the fear and darkness troubles them, please be near to them. I beg of you, please. They are the splendor.

Amen.

FORTY-FIVE

SATURDAY EVENINGS

✦✦✦✦✦✦✦✦✦

If it came cheap—our happiness and
freedom—
it wouldn't be worth having.

—*Rick Bass*

THE KIDS WERE OFF DOING other things. We were
fine with that, had even given permission for such things,
for that left time for two. So we took our plates laden with
grilled chicken and salad out to our cheap Adirondack Wal-
Mart chairs and we sat and ate, just the two of us. She had an

iPhone in her lap listening to the play-by-play of the Arkansas Razorbacks and I had a radio stationed nearby playing *The Sounds of Sinatra with Sid Mark*. We've learned to listen to two stations like that; it's one of the tricks of the long-married. *Touchdown, Arkansas!* mingled with *the wee small hours of the morning*. One might not think them compatible, but compatible was never our goal.

We talked about her Dad, how he loved Razorback football, and how he used to sit with friends in a detached garage and watch the game, but listen to it on the radio. She talked about being cut from such cloth and I said *I like that about you*. I wondered aloud what my kids would remember of me some day when they are grown and gone and enjoying a meal for one or two on a Saturday night. She said *they'll remember you listening to Sinatra*.

What's the secret to marriage, or parenting, or fatherhood, or any of it? I don't know. And I'm quite suspect of anyone claiming to know, even if they sold a million copies of a book about marriage or fatherhood or any of it. All I know is dusk-laden Saturday evenings when we steal away, just the two of us, and sit and remember where we came from and what we like about one another and what we hope they'll one day remember in the wee small hours.

There is no secret, only love.

NOTES

page 2. John Updike, *The Centaur* (New York: Fawcett, 1963).

page 103. http://www.pbs.org/newshour/bb/remember/jan-june09/updike_01-27.html